Lessons from David:

How to Be a Giant Killer

By

Andrew Wommack

Harrison House
Tulsa, OK

All scripture quotations are taken from the *King James Version* of the Bible.

17 16 15 14   10 9 8 7 6 5 4 3 2

Lessons from David: How to Be a Giant Killer
ISBN: 978-160683- 971-3
Copyright © 2014 by Andrew Wommack
P.O. Box 3333
Colorado Springs, CO 80934-333

Published by
Harrison House Publishers
Tulsa, OK 74145

Table of Contents

Introduction

Now all these things happened unto them for examples: and they are written for our admonition, upon whom the ends of the world are come.

1 Corinthians 10:11

The stories of people in the Old Testament were recorded as examples for us today. God's Word plainly reveals both the good and the bad about such highly regarded individuals as Moses, Abraham, and Elijah. We're not only told how the Lord was able to move mightily in their lives, but also how and why they failed. The purpose of these stories is to benefit you and me today.

Many people believe that the only way you can really learn something is through hard knocks. They think you have to experience your own hardships, situations, and circumstances. However, God wrote all of these things down in His Word so you and I wouldn't have to learn that way. Instead, we can learn through the experience of Bible characters—their successes and mistakes. Personally, I've found this to be a much better way.

David's life is full of lessons for us today. In this book, we'll be exploring the differences between David, Saul, and Absalom. We'll see the importance of David's heart attitude and relationship with God. We'll also reflect on the processes that led to his downfall and restoration.

It doesn't matter if you're succeeding in your calling, just starting out, or if you've failed miserably. David's life will encourage and inspire you to avoid temptation, trust God (even after you've fallen), and keep your heart sensitive to Him. The giants in your life won't stand a chance as these Lessons from David become your very own!

Chapter 1

Accept Responsibility

The early part of David's life was closely woven together with Saul's. Therefore, we can't really look into the life of David without first understanding some things about Saul.

Saul was…

A choice young man, and a goodly: and there was not among the children of Israel a goodlier person than he: from his shoulders and upward he was higher than any of the people.

1 Samuel 9:2

The tallest man in Israel only came up to Saul's shoulders. So for an Israelite, Saul was like a giant. However, he was also a very humble man. He started off being very little in his own eyes (1 Samuel 15:17), so the Lord chose him as king over the nation of Israel.

The people rallied to Saul and he was established as king. Saul sought the Lord during the first two or three years of his reign as king. God wrought some major deliverances through Saul and solidified the kingdom under him.

Lessons from David

Strange Fire

In 1 Samuel 13, Saul assembled the troops in preparation for battle against the Philistines. Samuel the prophet instructed Saul to wait seven days until he came to offer a sacrifice. Then after Samuel offered the sacrifice, the army of Israel would go into battle with God's blessing.

> *And he [Saul] tarried seven days, according to the set time that Samuel had appointed: but Samuel came not to Gilgal; and the people were scattered from him. And Saul said, Bring hither a burnt offering to me, and peace offerings. And he offered the burnt offering. And it came to pass, that as soon as he had made an end of offering the burnt offering, behold, Samuel came; and Saul went out to meet him, that he might salute him.*
>
> *1 Samuel 13:8-10; brackets mine*

Saul offered this sacrifice contrary to the instructions of God. The law prescribed that only priests could offer these sacrifices and petition the Lord like this. Saul stepped out of his position as king and attempted to assume the position of priest. He was a secular government official, not a priest. However, even a priest was required to offer sacrifices correctly according to God's instructions.

> *And Nadab and Abihu, the sons of Aaron [priests], took either of them his censer, and put fire therein, and put incense thereon, and offered strange fire before the LORD, which he*

commanded them not. And there went out fire from the L<small>ORD</small>,
and devoured them, and they died before the L<small>ORD</small>.

Leviticus 10:1-2; brackets mine

As priests, Nadab and Abihu were qualified to offer a sacrifice,
but they did not follow the proper order. Since they didn't do it the
way the Lord had prescribed, fire came out, and God struck them
dead. The Old Testament law was very strict in regard to these
things. Even if you were a priest, you had to perform your priestly
duties exactly the right way. Not only did Saul not know how to
properly offer the sacrifice, he was not even a priest. Obviously, he
committed a major sin in God's eyes.

Excuses, Excuses

As soon as Saul finished offering the sacrifice, Samuel showed
up (1 Samuel 13:10).

*And Samuel said, What hast thou done? And Saul said, Because
I saw that the people were scattered from me, and that thou
camest not within the days appointed, and that the Philistines
gathered themselves together at Michmash; therefore said I,
The Philistines will come down now upon me to Gilgal, and
I have not made supplication unto the* L<small>ORD</small>: *I forced myself
therefore, and offered a burnt offering.*

1 Samuel 13:11-12

Samuel reproved Saul for what he did and asked, "Why did
you do it?" Instead of humbling himself and saying, "I was wrong.

Please forgive me," Saul immediately began to justify himself and make excuses by saying, "The people were beginning to leave me."

Saul was a people pleaser. He was insecure and dependent on the approval of others. However, he tried to spiritualize it by saying, "I had to offer this sacrifice. I just couldn't go into battle without offering my sacrifice!" That may have been the custom and to some degree it may have been valid, but Saul was just using this as an excuse. Saul was not seeking God with all his heart. We know this to be true, based on the Lord's reaction.

If this had just been a mistake—a miscalculation—God wouldn't have responded to Saul the way He did. The Lord knew Saul's heart (1 Samuel 16:7), became very upset with him, and brought a severe punishment upon him. This shows that Saul knew exactly what he was doing. Yet, here he was, trying to explain himself away. This is a common practice. Instead of just admitting, "I blew it. Please forgive me," most people try to excuse themselves and shift the blame.

"It's My Fault, Lord"

David never blamed anyone else for his failures. He always took responsibility and admitted, "Lord, it's my fault." When David numbered the people, God became very angry (2 Samuel 24). After 70,000 Israelites died, the angel executing this judgment was about to enter Jerusalem. David fell on his face before the Lord and cried out:

Accept Responsibility

"Lo, I have sinned, and I have done wickedly: but these sheep, what have they done? let thine hand, I pray thee, be against me, and against my father's house."

2 Samuel 24:17

David didn't try to place the blame on others like Saul did by saying, "It's their fault. They made me do it!" No, he took responsibility and shouldered the blame himself. This is one of the character traits that made David a man after God's own heart (1 Samuel 13:14).

Victim or Victor?

David made some serious mistakes. When the Bible talks about having a pure heart—a perfect heart—it doesn't mean that you never sin. It's talking about how you respond when you do sin. When you make a mistake, do you blame other people? Are you someone who refuses to accept the truth that it's your fault that you're in a mess? Do you always blame things on the past, your dysfunctional family, your circumstances or other factors? Are you a victim or a victor?

This victim mentality or attitude is very popular in our society. It's an attempt to dodge responsibility and blame others. This was Saul's attitude. People with this attitude won't survive, be blessed, or reach their full potential. If you want to be a person after God's own heart, take a lesson from David and start accepting responsibility when you're wrong. Stop making excuses and blaming others! Be a victor, not a victim!

I pray that the Holy Spirit will quicken this truth to you and help you apply it to your situation. If you haven't accepted that the predicament your find yourself in is your fault and you're still blaming everything and everyone else, you need to accept responsibility. Why is this so important? Because you have to accept responsibility in order to be in control and change things.

If other people and circumstances have made you the mess that you are, then you can never change. There are many things you cannot change. You cannot change the family you were born into, the color of your skin, where you grew up, other people, or a myriad of other outside factors. There are many circumstances and aspects of your environment that you have absolutely no control over. However, if you will accept responsibility and say, "Regardless of what's been done to me, it's the way I have responded to it that has made me the way I am. It's my fault, Lord. Please forgive me," then you can change. **You** are the only one **you** can change. In order to stop being a victim and start being a victor, you must accept responsibility for your own messes.

You're Foolish!

And Samuel said to Saul, Thou hast done foolishly.

1 Samuel 13:13

Saul had disobeyed God. He tried to rationalize and explain away what he did by saying, "The people made me do it. I had to offer this sacrifice because I didn't want to go to war without asking God's favor." Saul had a million excuses.

You can try to make it look good but if you disobey God, you're foolish. It doesn't matter what you say, how you justify it, or what the extenuating circumstances are, disobedience to God is wrong! There is no such thing as "situational ethics." There is right and wrong. You need to quit blaming somebody else and accept the fact that if you disobey God, you're foolish.

> *Thou hast done foolishly: thou hast not kept the commandment of the LORD thy God, which he commanded thee: for now would the LORD have established thy kingdom upon Israel for ever.*
>
> *1 Samuel 13:13*

This statement conflicts with many people's theology. Many folks think that since God knows the end from the beginning, He also controls everything that happens in between. Since God is all-knowing and all-powerful, they believe that only what He wills comes to pass on the earth. That kind of belief makes the Lord responsible for all the evil in the world. After all, it couldn't happen unless He "willed" or "allowed" it. This kind of false teaching is popularly called, "the sovereignty of God." I confront and refute this wrong doctrine head on in my teaching by the same name.

God's Original Plan

If we applied these faulty assumptions to Saul, people would say, "God knew exactly who Saul was and what he would do. He knew that Saul was going to fail. Therefore, Saul was just a temporary pick in God's true plan. All along, the Lord planned for Saul to fail so He could raise David up. This was God's sovereign plan."

God, speaking through the prophet Samuel, clearly refutes this assumption in His words to Saul found in 1 Samuel 13:13: "If you would have obeyed Me and not done your own thing, and trusted Me and waited just one more hour until Samuel showed up, I would have established your kingdom upon Israel forever" (paraphrase mine). This means that David was not God's first choice.

The Lord didn't choose Saul as a mere interim, temporary king over Israel, until the real person He wanted—David—could come of age and take over. No! God's Word plainly reveals that His first choice was Saul. If Saul had cooperated with the Lord, He would have established his kingdom over the nation of Israel forever. This means we would have never even heard of David.

This is a little hard for people who really know the Bible to comprehend. Why? Because David is everywhere throughout God's Word. He was blessed. As a matter of fact, the southern kingdom of the nation of Israel was preserved and lasted longer than the northern ten tribes because the Lord was honoring David. He spared his descendants because of David.

Today we speak of the "sure mercies of David." God made an oath and a covenant that He would establish the throne of David's kingdom forever. This was ultimately fulfilled through Messiah— Jesus Christ—who was called "the Son of David." Prophecies spoke of the Messiah coming out of the tribe of Judah, David's tribe.

But 1 Samuel 13:13 makes it very clear that David wasn't God's first choice. If Saul had obeyed the Lord, we would be talking about the "sure mercies of Saul" today. The Messiah would have come out of the tribe of Benjamin, Saul's tribe. We never would have heard of David. There would never have been a Solomon. There might have been others who did equal or even greater things, but David wasn't God's original plan.

"An Expected End"

One of the most important lessons we can learn from the life of David is that God chose David as a result of Saul's disobedience.

For now would the LORD have established thy kingdom upon Israel for ever. But now thy kingdom shall not continue: the LORD hath sought him a man after his own heart, and the LORD hath commanded him to be captain over his people, because thou hast not kept that which the LORD commanded thee.

1 Samuel 13:13-14

The Lord sought out David *after* Saul rejected Him. This instance took place in the second year of Saul's reign (1 Samuel 13:1). At the end of Saul's forty-year reign (Acts 13:21), David became king when he was thirty years old (2 Samuel 5:4). This meant that David wasn't even born when Saul rejected God and received notice of God's judgment through the prophet Samuel. David was born eight years later. David wasn't God's first choice—Saul was!

Just because you have stumbled upon God's will for your life and have begun to fulfill it, that doesn't mean you'll automatically finish the course. Just because you can see His calling, anointing, and blessing on your life, do not think you can't thwart it. That isn't God's plan for you, but you can thwart God's plan.

As far as God is concerned, He's willing and planning for you to prosper.

For I know the thoughts that I think toward you, saith the LORD, thoughts of peace, and not of evil, to give you an expected end.

Jeremiah 29:11

God has a good plan for every individual. It's a plan that will give you an "expected end"—a predicted future of success. The Lord has a plan and purpose for everyone. He desires for every person to fulfill his individual destiny, but this doesn't automatically or sovereignly come to pass. You can thwart God's plan for your life, as did Saul.

Nobody who truly believes that the Bible is the Word of God can say, "Well, God knew Saul was going to do all of these things. He was just a fill-in for David, God's true plan." No! Saul was the one God really planned to lead Israel. That's exactly what the Word says!

Grace Can Be Voided

The example of Saul can serve as a warning to all of us. The Lord has a plan for each one of us that is by grace—it's not based on our performance—but we do have to cooperate with that plan. Even though we don't deserve our God-given destiny, there are things we can do that will hinder or stop it from coming to pass in our lives.

Accept Responsibility

So take heed and beware! You can't just take the grace of God, His blessing, and His calling on your life for granted. You need to persevere.

Paul understood and cooperated with this truth.

For I am the least of the apostles...but by the grace of God I am what I am.

1 Corinthians 15:9-10

Paul's calling was by God's grace. He didn't deserve it. But Paul went on to say...

And his grace which was bestowed upon me was not in vain.

1 Corinthians 15:10

In other words, God can give grace to you, but you can void it. The Lord has a plan for your life, but you can invalidate it.

His grace...was not in vain; but I laboured more abundantly than they all: yet not I, but the grace of God which was with me.

1 Corinthians 15:10

Paul was saying that the Lord—by grace—chose him. Paul wasn't really seeking God at the time God chose him. He was hunting down, persecuting, and killing Christians. According to the Lord himself, Paul was kicking "against the pricks" (Acts 9:5). Paul wasn't chosen because of any great virtue on his part. It was a grace decision. Yet Paul was saying that he could have made it vain and voided the grace of God. Thankfully he didn't, and instead he responded by faith to God's grace and "laboured more abundantly."

Lessons from David

A Sobering Thought

Just like Saul, God has a purpose and plan for each and every one of us. Even after Saul sinned in 1 Samuel 13, God didn't immediately take him out of the kingship.

For the gifts and calling of God are without repentance.

Romans 11:29

Saul remained king until the day of his death. His kingdom however, instead of being a blessing, turned into a burden for the nation of Israel. Saul oppressed and took advantage of the people. He was tormented, did terrible things, and basically went crazy. He destroyed his son Jonathan's life. Saul certainly did not realize his full potential.

God's plan for your life is by grace, but you must cooperate with that grace by faith. Like Saul, you can stop God's plan and blessing from fully materializing (1 Samuel 13:13-14). Now that's a sobering thought!

Chapter 2
Do You Qualify?

Saul's failure gave David a chance. David was God's second choice. He never would have even come to the surface if Saul hadn't botched it up. This speaks volumes to me! Even though the Lord has used me in a mighty way, I certainly don't feel like I was His first choice.

I used to serve as an usher in Katherine Kuhlman's meetings. Katherine had a powerful, world-renowned ministry of healing. I saw some of the most astounding miracles I've ever seen in my life at her meetings. She made a huge impact for the kingdom of God. But I heard Katherine say on more than one occasion that she wasn't God's first, second, or even third choice. In her own dramatic way, she continued right on down the line, saying she wasn't even God's fourth or fifth choice. She would openly admit that she wasn't the best person to do the job, but then she'd turn right around to the preachers in the audience and chastise them by saying, "God called some of you to do what I'm doing, but you wouldn't bear up under the criticism and persecution." She would just let them have it!

This has always encouraged me because I have never felt like I was the best qualified or most suited person to do what I'm doing. But one of the things I've learned from the life of David is that God doesn't necessarily choose the silver vessel. He chooses the surrendered one. The Lord is more interested in our *availability* than our *ability*.

God's Qualifications

You may feel like you have it all together, but I'm a hick from Texas. I've had people make fun of me. They've talked about my "hick" voice and how I sound like that old television character, Gomer Pyle. I don't get upset about that. In fact, I don't particularly like my voice either. If I were God, I wouldn't have chosen me. When He chose me and started putting the things He's told me to do in my heart, I just thought, *God, I'm not qualified. I'm not good enough!* But then I read His list of qualifications found in 1 Corinthians:

> *For ye see your calling, brethren, how that not many wise men after the flesh, not many mighty, not many noble, are called: but God hath chosen the foolish things of the world to confound the wise; and God hath chosen the weak things of the world to confound the things which are mighty.*
>
> *1 Corinthians 1:26-27*

When I saw this, I thought, *Hey, I qualify! That's me!*

Do You Qualify?

And base things of the world, and things which are despised,
hath God chosen, yea, and things which are not, to bring to
nought things that are: that no flesh should glory in his presence

1 Corinthians 1:28-29

God doesn't choose the way man does. He looks on the heart. Saul started out with a tender heart, so God gave him the opportunity. He chose him. But when his heart changed, God forsook him and turned away from him.

A Yielded Heart

As New Testament believers, God will never leave us nor forsake us (Hebrews 13:5). However, He won't continue to promote us if we get an evil heart. The Lord will still love us and accept us, but He won't open doors for us. God will not promote a rotten attitude. We can stop the blessing and promotion of God from coming in our life. He won't leave us or forsake us the way He did with Saul, but we can certainly hinder, stop, and thwart His blessing in our life.

Therefore, you need to recognize that God is looking for a humble heart. He's looking at the attitude of your heart. Just like with David, the Lord is seeking people after His own heart. This encourages me.

God didn't choose David because David was the tallest. Saul was the tallest in the entire nation, but David was the runt of the litter. Saul was a tough looking, masculine man. He was probably weathered from being out in the sun and wind. David was ruddy and had a beautiful complexion (1 Samuel 16:12). He had a countenance that was enjoyable to look at. In other words, he was a "Mama's Boy." David was nice looking, but not the kind of guy you would pick to go out and fight a battle. People look on the outward appearance, but God looks on the heart (1 Samuel 16:7).

Through studying the life of David, I've learned that the Lord isn't concerned with external things. He is not concerned with my skills, abilities, or whether or not I have charisma. He looks at my heart, whether I will trust Him or not. Once I saw this, I thought, *God, I may not have the education, the polish, the talent, or the looks. I may not have the strength or natural ability that other people do, but I have a heart. And I choose to commit my heart to seeking You as much as anybody ever has!* That's been my pursuit. I'm not saying that I have fully attained it, but I have consistently and honestly sought to love God in spirit and in truth with my whole heart. The Lord has honored that. He has blessed me and has opened up doors in my life and ministry.

I've seen many people's lives changed by the power of God's Word and the Holy Spirit. I've seen blind eyes and deaf ears opened, terminal diseases healed, and people raised from the dead—including my own son! What a blessing! Why did those things come to pass? Because, I started seeking God with my whole heart. I don't have the ability in my hands to heal or raise anyone from the dead, but I can yield my heart to Him and He can use me to work miracles. God wants to use you too. It's all about your heart.

Seek Him Wholeheartedly!

Even though David wasn't God's first choice, look what the Lord was able to do with him. He made an impact. Nearly four thousand years later, we're still learning from the life of David and talking about what a great man he was. Many people's lives were transformed by the life of David. God used him to transform the Israelites from a rag tag bunch of tribal groups into a nation. They gained prominence and were established as a nation that is still in existence today. Great things happened!

David wasn't God's first choice. He didn't have all of the qualifications the world might look for in a leader, but he yielded his whole heart to God. The Lord chose him, and God's "Plan B" was better than any of us could have ever imagined His "Plan A" being.

The good news is that God can do the same for you. You may not have it all together. In fact, you may consider yourself weak, base, and despised. Well, according to 1 Corinthians 1:26-29, you qualify! All you have to do is yield your heart to Him.

I probably wasn't the Lord's first choice. But I've chosen God and because of that, He's chosen to use me. Maybe someone else was better qualified, but nonetheless He's using me. I just praise Him for the opportunity. God is awesome!

You don't have to be perfect for the Lord to use you. You just have to seek Him with your whole heart. If you hunger and thirst for God, you will be filled (Matthew 5:6)!

Lessons from David:

Chapter 3

Obedience Is Better

Thus saith the LORD *of hosts, I remember that which Amalek did to Israel, how he laid wait for him in the way, when he came up from Egypt. Now go and smite Amalek, and utterly destroy all that they have, and spare them not; but slay both man and woman, infant and suckling, ox and sheep, camel and ass.*

1 Samuel 15:2-3

This was God's commission through Samuel to Saul. Amalek had come out and fought against the Israelites when they were vulnerable and on their way out of Egypt (Exodus 17:8-14). Now that Israel was a kingdom and had a king, God wanted vengeance on the Amalekites.

This may seem harsh to us today because truthfully speaking, vengeance isn't acceptable New Covenant behavior. Now that Jesus has come, He has made a huge difference. In my book entitled, *The True Nature of God*, I contrast and harmonize the difference between how God acted in the Old Testament as compared to the New Testament. This teaching really shines the light on how the Lord can be "the same yesterday, and today, and forever" (Hebrews 13:8), and yet appear so different in the two testaments. This teaching will really set you free!

In the Old Testament, groups of people who had given themselves over to idolatry and immorality were like cancers in the body of humankind. If left untreated, that sickness would spread quickly to the rest of the body. As terrible as it is to amputate someone's hand, arm, or leg, loss of limb is still superior to the death of the entire person. Sometimes you just have to cut the diseased part out in order to save the rest of the body. This was exactly what God—in His love and mercy—was instructing the Israelites to do. By utterly destroying these men, women, children, and animals, they were cutting out a cancer that threatened to kill the rest of humankind.

Before Jesus came so people could be born again, transformed, and delivered of demons, there were entire societies that were so given over to the devil that they were demon possessed. Men, women, children, and even their animals were demon possessed. There is much archaeological evidence—statues, writings, and the like—that establishes this as fact. The sin of these societies was gross beyond what we can even imagine in our society today, and our sin is pretty gross in many ways. These people were participating on a wide scale in bestiality, sodomy, child sacrifice, and all these kinds of things, to the extent that they couldn't be cured. There was no cure before Jesus came. So although the command given to Saul constituted an act of judgment against specific individuals, it was also an act of mercy upon the world, as the actions of Israel were meant to literally cut this cancer out and destroy it.

"The People…"

Saul was given this command to destroy all of the Amalekites—men, women, children, and animals—but he didn't do it. He saved the king and brought him back with the best of the sheep, oxen, and cattle. When Samuel arrived, Saul claimed that he had done the will of the Lord (1 Samuel 15:13). But Samuel asked:

What meaneth then this bleating of the sheep in mine ears, and the lowing of the oxen which I hear?

1 Samuel 15:14

In other words, Samuel was asking, "If you have truly done the Lord's will, why am I hearing these animals? I told you to destroy everything—men, women, children, and animals!"

And Saul said, 'They have brought them from the Amalekites."

1 Samuel 15:15

There he was placing the blame on others again and saying, "The people made me do this!"

For the people spared the best of the sheep and of the oxen, to sacrifice unto the LORD thy God; and the rest we have utterly destroyed. Then Samuel said unto Saul, Stay, and I will tell thee what the LORD hath said to me this night. And he said unto him, Say on. And Samuel said, 'When thou wast little in thine own sight, wast thou not made the head of the tribes of Israel, and the LORD anointed thee king over Israel?'

1 Samuel 15:15-17

Samuel was exposing the root of Saul's sin. He said, "When you were little in your own eyes, God anointed and promoted you. But when you were lifted up, you became independent, started doing things your own way, and chose not to do what God said. Instead of killing these animals—like you were instructed to do—you decided to bring them back and sacrifice them. It was when you became arrogant that God rejected you."

Pride & Humility

Pride goeth before destruction, and an haughty spirit before a fall.

Proverbs 16:18

God resisteth the proud, and giveth grace to the humble.

1 Peter 5:5

Humility is necessary to walk with God.

He [God] hath shown thee, O man, what is good; and what doth the LORD require of thee, but to…walk humbly with thy God.

Micah 6:8; brackets mine

You must walk humbly in order to walk with God. This is a lesson we can learn from David. David was a humble man. At times, he messed up royally and committed terrible sins, but he didn't try to shift the blame onto anyone else when he was reproved. He shouldered the blame himself, repented, and lay before the Lord. David was a humble man.

Humility doesn't mean you do everything perfectly. It doesn't mean you don't sin. Humility means that you have a heart that is sensitive toward the Lord. Even though you might act like you've lost your mind and gone crazy sometimes, you genuinely love God.

Humility is different than arrogance. Saul got caught up in arrogance. Pride isn't only thinking that you are better than everyone else. Pride is essentially being self-reliant instead of God-reliant. This attitude of independence is one of Satan's biggest inroads into our lives.

<u>Only</u> by pride cometh contention.

Proverbs 13:10; emphasis mine

I have a booklet entitled, *Self-centeredness, The Source of all Grief,* that expounds more on this. The only thing that makes people mad is their self-centeredness or self-reliance. This is Satan's major beachhead in our lives. If you want to shut the devil out of your life, begin to prosper, and see the blessings of God work, you need to walk humbly with God. You won't find God until you come to the end of yourself. At the end of yourself is where you'll meet Him!

Stay Small in Your Own Sight

Samuel told Saul, "When you were little in your own sight, you were made the head of the tribes of Israel." When Saul was humble, God promoted him.

At one time, I was a member of a church that had started in someone's basement. In about two-year's time, it grew to 300 people. It outgrew its little church facility and took over the large grocery store building next door. On opening day, there were about 500 people in attendance. The church had nearly doubled. It was exciting to be part of what was going on. People were praising God, but they were also praising the pastor and themselves. They were saying, "Look who we are!" They were giving a tremendous amount of attention to what they had done. This just struck me wrong.

People were standing up and prophesying, "This church is going to explode! It's going to do this and that!" Then the Lord spoke to me this exact passage of scripture, 1 Samuel 15:17. So I went against the flow that day by standing up and saying, "It's wonderful what God has done, but all this started when we were little in our own eyes and humble before the Lord. If we get into pride and arrogance, all this can leave just as quickly as it came."

I wasn't real popular after that, but that's exactly what happened. The church went through a really terrible time for a while. The pastor ended up getting into some things, got divorced and left the ministry. The church fell apart. Since then, it has resurrected under another pastor and is now doing better than ever before. This principle applies to individuals as well as churches.

Years ago, there was a major media minister who fell into sexual sin. His sin was made public and finally the minister had to deal with it on his Sunday program. I watched and listened to what he had to say, trying to figure out how something like this could happen. As he confessed, he spoke of how he had fallen into pride and claimed achievements that had come because of God's goodness as his own accomplishments. He said he had over $8 million dollars coming in every month. He was on more television stations than any other person in history. He said, "I'm reaching more people than Jesus ever did." He also went on to say, "I thought I could do anything."

At that moment, I saw very clearly why this man fell. He was no longer humble and dependent on God. He thought he was the one causing all this prosperity in his ministry.

From the life of David, we learn that we must walk humbly with God. Saul, David's predecessor, was the Lord's first choice to lead Israel, but he didn't continue walking with God because he became lifted up in pride, did his own thing, and disobeyed.

"It's Not My Fault!"

And Samuel said, When thou wast little in thine own sight, wast thou not made the head of the tribes of Israel, and the Lord anointed thee king over Israel? And the Lord sent thee on a journey, and said, Go and utterly destroy the sinners the Amalekites, and fight against them until they be consumed. Wherefore then didst thou not obey the voice of the Lord, but didst fly upon the spoil, and didst evil in the sight of the Lord?

1 Samuel 15:17-19

Samuel reproved Saul, but Saul kept on saying, "It's not my fault! You don't understand. I did obey God!" But he didn't.

Lessons from David:

And Saul said unto Samuel, Yea, I have obeyed the voice of the LORD, and have gone the way which the LORD sent me, and have brought Agag the king of Amalek, and have utterly destroyed the Amalekites. But the people took of the spoil....

1 Samuel 15:20-21

Saul's cry was, "It's not my fault! The people did this. They took the spoils of sheep and oxen." But Saul was the king. He was the one responsible. He knew what they had done. He could have commanded them to obey God's directions. The Lord wouldn't have held him guilty if the people had truly done all of this. However, Saul was the one who did it, and the people had his full approval.

The people took of the spoil, sheep and oxen, the chief of the things which should have been utterly destroyed.

1 Samuel 15:21

This verse clearly reveals that Saul knew these things "should have been utterly destroyed" (1 Samuel 15:21). He knew what the people were doing. So Saul attempted to justify himself by saying that he and the people took these things "to sacrifice unto the LORD thy God in Gilgal" (1 Samuel 15:21).

And Samuel said, Hath the LORD as great delight in burnt offerings and sacrifices, as in obeying the voice of the LORD? Behold, to obey is better than sacrifice, and to hearken than the fat of rams.

1 Samuel 15:22

When God tells you to do something, it's not open to

negotiation. You don't need to "interpret" His command. You just need to do what God has told you to do.

Obey God

I've had people say to me, "God has told me to come to Charis Bible College. I know I'm supposed to come, and I believe I'm supposed to come now. But it's only a couple more years before I can take an early retirement. If I wait until then I could have that much more money than if I go now. Also, it's not a good time to sell my house right now. The market should be better, if I just wait a year or two." So they rationalize things and don't obey God. They lean on their own understanding and wonder why everything starts heading south. They tell me, "I don't understand why nothing is working. I just can't figure out what's happening!"

I answer, "Well, you aren't obeying God."

"Oh, no! I am obeying God. I'm going to come, but I just have to wait until this and that happens." They try to explain it away, but that's not what God has told them to do.

The Lord told Saul to kill all of the people and animals there, when he fought against them. Instead, he decided to bring them and offer them as sacrifices before God. That's not what the Lord told him to do!

And Samuel said, Hath the Lord as great delight in burnt offerings and sacrifices, as in obeying the voice of the Lord?

Lessons from David:

Behold, to obey is better than sacrifice, and to hearken than the fat of rams.

1 Samuel 15:22

You can't make deals with God and say, "Lord, I know You told me to give this money right now, but I need it. I have something I really want to spend it on. I'll tell You what. I'll just take this money and get what I want now, and then I'll double it and give You that much later." No. That's not pleasing to the Lord. He wants you to obey Him and do what He told you to do—when He told you to do it!

To obey is better than sacrifice.

1 Samuel 15:22

What Are You Allowing?

Samuel continued by saying:

For rebellion is as the sin of witchcraft, and stubbornness is as iniquity and idolatry.

1 Samuel 15:23

Strong statements, indeed! Not doing what God has told you to do is rebellion and stubbornness is as iniquity and idolatry. We just haven't placed that kind of stigma on rebellion and stubbornness! I'm sure you wouldn't tolerate witchcraft in your home. If your children came home with an Ouija board, started putting séances together, or tried casting spells, you'd be all over them like a coat of wet paint, declaring, "Not in this house! As long as I'm breathing,

I will not allow witchcraft or idolatry in this house!" You wouldn't let them make some little graven image and begin to worship it. But there are many parents who just allow their kids to go through rebellion, be stubborn, talk back to them, and disrespect authority and not even think anything of it. They reason, *Well, they're just teenagers. That's normal!*

Now don't get me wrong! I'm not saying that you can, or should completely control your children. But I am saying that if you discern rebellion, you ought to resist it. If you detect stubbornness, you should be doing something about it. Many people just don't place that kind of importance upon this. They argue, "But rebellion is normal!" No, it's not. First Samuel 15:23 tells us it's the same as allowing witchcraft into your home!

Listen to the Lord!

If you permitted a poisonous snake to live in your house, maybe you could go for a day, a week, a month, or a year without it biting you. But if you allow that snake to stay in your home, sooner or later it could take your life or the life of one of your kids. You wouldn't live like that—it's not worth the risk! Well, many people do even worse by allowing rebellion and stubbornness to have a place in their life and home. We know we aren't doing things exactly the way God has told us to. We're aware of the fact that we are often slow to obey. God has to badger us and drive us into a corner in order to get us to do something. You might say, "But that's the way that I am. I'm just not quick to obey!" Then you're rebellious and stubborn and according to 1 Samuel 15:23, that's witchcraft, iniquity, and idolatry!

This was why Saul was rejected and David was chosen. If you want to be a David instead of a Saul, quit disobeying God. Stop being rebellious and stubborn. Listen to the Lord and obey Him quickly and fully from your heart.

Chapter 4

Move On!

For rebellion is as the sin of witchcraft, and stubbornness is as iniquity and idolatry. Because thou hast rejected the word of the LORD, he hath also rejected thee from being king.

And Saul said unto Samuel, I have sinned: for I have transgressed the commandment of the LORD, and thy words: because I feared the people, and obeyed their voice.

1 Samuel 15:23-24

S aul finally admitted, "Alright, I'm wrong. But I'm wrong because I feared the people and they forced me into it!" He still didn't take direct responsibility.

If you want to be a Saul, then dodge responsibility and say, "I'm this way because of my dysfunctional family, the color of my skin, my lack of education, or this bad thing that happened to me. You don't understand. I was abused as a child!" Saul had a victim mentality. This mentality leads to destruction. If you want to be a David—someone after God's own heart—then start accepting responsibility for your own wrongs and quit blaming everybody else.

Quit fearing people! Saul said, "I was afraid of the people. They coerced me into it!" He was the king. He was God's appointed leader. He had the authority. But instead of doing the right thing, he let the tail wag the dog.

"Honor Me, Please!"

Saul went on to say:

Now therefore, I pray thee, pardon my sin, and turn again with me, that I may worship the LORD.

And Samuel said unto Saul, I will not return with thee: for thou hast rejected the word of the LORD, and the LORD hath rejected thee from being king over Israel. And as Samuel turned about to go away, he laid hold upon the skirt of his mantle, and it rent. And Samuel said unto him, The LORD hath rent the kingdom of Israel from thee this day, and hath given it to a neighbour of thine, that is better than thou. And also the Strength of Israel will not lie nor repent: for he is not a man, that he should repent.

Then he [Saul] said, I have sinned: yet honour me now, I pray thee, before the elders of my people, and before Israel, and turn again with me, that I may worship the LORD thy God.

1 Samuel 15:25-30; brackets mine

Samuel told Saul that the Lord had rejected him. This meant that Saul would ultimately lose the kingdom. His children and family would no longer be royalty; he would lose everything. Yet he wanted Samuel to offer a sacrifice to the Lord with him, so the people would stay with him. He wasn't as concerned about losing the Lord's approval as he was about what the people thought. This was one of Saul's major flaws and it is a distinguishing characteristic of pride and insecurity. The fear of man is a snare (Proverbs 29:25). David's outlook was the opposite of this.

The last verse of this chapter says:

And Samuel came no more to see Saul until the day of his death: nevertheless Samuel mourned for Saul: and the LORD repented that he had made Saul king over Israel.

1 Samuel 15:35

"How Long?"

And the LORD said unto Samuel, How long wilt thou mourn for Saul, seeing I have rejected him from reigning over Israel? fill thine horn with oil, and go, I will send thee to Jesse the Bethlehemite: for I have provided me a king among his sons.

1 Samuel 16:1

Saul was God's first choice to run the kingdom. God regretted that He had made Saul king and then had to reject him. But once that was done—once Saul made his choice—God moved on. God wasn't living in the past, sitting there sulking, pouting, and brooding over all these things. He said, "I have provided Myself another king from among the sons of Jesse." The Lord got up and went on with Plan B!

Lessons from David:

God is more concerned with getting His plan done than He is about mourning what could have or should have been. On the other hand, Samuel mourned for Saul constantly. Finally, the Lord asked him, "How long are you going to mourn for Saul?"

This can be a major problem today. People see a move of God and they just want to build three tabernacles and camp there (Matthew 17:4). Yet, it's time to move on. In the wilderness, there was a cloud that hovered over the tabernacle. When the cloud moved, the Israelites had to get up and move (Exodus 40:36-38). They couldn't stay there. They had to move on and follow God. He had a place for them to go.

God has a purpose for your life. Along the way, you'll encounter individuals who fail and fall away from Him. They may be people you've loved and respected. A church leader you idolized may fall into sexual sin, misappropriate money, or otherwise fail. I can't tell you how many people I've seen just fall apart when the person they were leaning on failed. You need to move on and continue with your life in Christ. Don't let this stop you!

When It's Time to Go

Samuel was beginning to fall into this trap of mourning and stagnation until God spoke to him. "How long are you going to mourn? I've rejected Saul. Now you reject him too!" That may sound harsh in light of the New Testament. Know that God will never totally forsake us—but He can move on to Plan B. God can say, "Alright, I'll use you to the degree that you're usable, that you allow Me to use you, but I'm not going to let My kingdom suffer. I'll raise up somebody else to get the job done!" He'll move on. If God moves on, He takes His anointing and puts it on another person. He takes His anointing from one church and puts it on another. Don't just sit there and die along with that church. If the glory cloud has lifted, move on! Do what God has told you to do!

God told Samuel:

Fill thine horn with oil, and go.

1 Samuel 16:1

In the Old Testament, oil symbolized the Holy Spirit. When they anointed priests and kings with oil, the power of the Holy Spirit came upon them and energized them to be used of God. So basically, the Lord was telling Samuel to quit mourning over Saul. "Forget the things that are behind and look forward to what's next! Be full of the Holy Ghost and go do what I've told you to do." That's a powerful word for you and me today.

There have been times in my life when I was just devastated. Sometimes it was a result of a tragedy, other times it was just a result of negative things that had happened. In these times, my natural tendency was to lose my motivation. I just wanted to sit there and cry, "Oh God, how could this have happened?" During those times the Lord has told me, "Get up, fill your horn with oil and go. Move forward with the vision and mission I've given you!" The message God has given me to share is too important for me to sit down and grieve over something bad that's happened.

On other occasions, something has occurred that was so

wonderful, I just wanted to stay there. When I first started in ministry, I pastored some small groups of people. I laid my life down for them, because I truly loved them. Even though I struggled because my calling and anointing was to be a teacher—not a pastor—I was doing it at the time because the Lord had led me to. When the time came and God was moving me on, I didn't want to leave those people. I was willing to put the rest of the plans and goals for my life on hold so I could just stay there and be a blessing to those people. But God told me, "Fill your horn with oil and go!"

It's not always something negative that's holding us back. Sometimes it could be a wonderful experience that you're afraid to leave. Either way, when the cloud of God starts moving, fill your horn with oil and go!

More Hands in Heaven

I had some friends who started out in a Presbyterian church. They began ministering to a group of college-aged kids in their home and that eventually grew into a church. However, when it was time to transition from being part of this Presbyterian church to pastoring the new church, it was challenging. Although they loved the people in the other church, they knew God was guiding them to step out and lead this new one. The husband was pretty much ready to go for it, but the wife was really struggling with leaving their old church and the people they had grown to love so much.

As they prayed about this, holding hands with friends around a kitchen table, the Lord gave the wife a word. He said, "Sometimes you have to let go of the hands you're holding onto so that there will be more hands around My table in heaven." In other words, sometimes you have to sacrifice certain relationships in order to go on and fulfill what God has called you to do. We need to be willing to do this. Whether it's something negative that's causing us to grieve or something positive that we would rather not leave, when God leads us to move on, we need to fill our horn with oil and go!

Lessons from David:

Chapter 5

A Heart for God

Samuel went to Bethlehem and found Jesse. He told him that God had sent him to anoint a king from among his sons. "Therefore, call your house together immediately!" So Jesse's sons came before the prophet.

And it came to pass, when they were come, that he looked on Eliab, and said, Surely the LORD's anointed is before him.

1 Samuel 16:6

Eliab was David's oldest brother. He was the biggest, strongest, and probably the meanest and toughest too. As a result, Samuel was looking at him and remembering Saul. Saul had been head-and-shoulders taller than anyone else in Israel. He had been the oldest son of his father. The first person that God had chosen to be king was this hunk of a man, so Samuel was just supposing that this was the way it was going to be. When he saw Eliab—the oldest, strongest, tallest, toughest-looking son of Jesse—Samuel commented, "Surely the Lord's anointed is before me!"

But the LORD said unto Samuel, Look not on his countenance, or on the height of his stature; because I have refused him: for

Lessons from David:

the LORD seeth not as man seeth; for man looketh on the outward appearance, but the LORD looketh on the heart.

1 Samuel 16:7

What an awesome truth! God doesn't look at us the way man does. David was the runt of the litter. As a matter of fact, David's own father didn't think that he had a chance, so he didn't even put David's name in the hat. Jesse had eight sons, but he only brought the eldest seven as candidates for this job of king of Israel. He thought, *David doesn't stand a chance. Never in a million years would he be picked!* David was the youngest. He didn't look like king material. But God doesn't look at things the way man does.

How Do You Evaluate?

When you evaluate people or physical things, you can't just evaluate them based on the way they look. Neither can you read a book by simply looking at its cover. (If you had, you wouldn't be reading these words right now!) God looks on the inside and sees differently than man sees. You need to keep this in mind when you evaluate others.

This is also true for when other people evaluate you. You don't need to buy into their evaluation because they may be merely looking on your outward appearance. If you're born again, you are a brand-new person on the inside. You are a king and priest on the inside. You are a son of God. You're anointed. You're powerful. One third of you is "wall-to-wall" Holy Ghost! Don't let other people's opinions and evaluations of who you are in the natural realm (your education, looks, talents, voice, and abilities) limit you!

Our society puts so much emphasis on outward appearance. People are starving themselves to death because they believe that skinny is beautiful and fat is ugly. I'm not saying that I think chubby is beautiful (though some cultures do), but I am saying that we put too much attention on that. Just because you're overweight, not too good looking, or don't have the greatest education, doesn't mean that God can't use you. Remember 1 Corinthians 1:26-29? God chooses the base, weak, despised, and foolish things to confound the wise. God sees things differently than man does.

Don't accept evaluations based on external things only. If you have a relationship with God, that qualifies you. The Lord has put all kinds of good things inside you. You just need to start seeing yourself the way God sees you.

Is Your Name in the Hat?

Then Jesse called Abinadab, and made him pass before Samuel. And he said, Neither hath the LORD chosen this. Then Jesse made Shammah to pass by. And he said, Neither hath the LORD chosen this.

1 Samuel 16:8-9

Finally, all seven of the sons present had passed before the prophet. Samuel said, "Nope! None of these are him!" As far as Samuel knew, these were all of the sons of Jesse. Yet he was sensitive enough to God to know that none of them were the right one. Since he knew that God had said that one of Jesse's sons would be the next king and obviously none of these were him, Samuel asked, "Are these all the sons you have?"

Jesse answered:

There remaineth yet the youngest, and, behold, he keepeth the sheep. And Samuel said unto Jesse, Send and fetch him: for we will not sit down till he come hither.

1 Samuel 16:11

At one time, my brother owned a small mechanical shop. He was behind on some bills and his creditors called him, asking for money. One fellow in particular just got mean and vicious and tried to intimidate him. Basically, my brother told him, "Look, here's the way I do it. I put everybody's name in a hat. Then I just draw names out and pay bills until I run out of money. I just haven't picked your name out of the hat yet."

The guy snarled, "Well, I want my money!"

My brother responded, "If you keep bothering me, I'm going to take your name out of the hat!" The guy stopped calling.

Jesse didn't even put David's name in the hat. He didn't think enough of his youngest son to bring him before the prophet. But Samuel said, "He must be the one! Therefore, none of us are going to sit down until David comes."

God Is Looking

Back then, they couldn't just call David on his cell phone. There were no cars to drive out to the pasture to get him. David may have been quite a way off in the wilderness, off somewhere keeping the sheep. It must have taken someone traveling on foot round-trip at least an hour to bring David back. So when Samuel said, "None of us will sit down until he comes," it put a real urgency upon the messenger to retrieve David as quickly as possible. It was a pain for all of them to just stand there until David came.

This also showed a tremendous amount of honor and respect. By this time, Samuel had recognized that David was the chosen one, regardless of what he might look like. The prophet was going by the Word of the Lord in honoring David.

Out in the wilderness, David knew what was happening. He knew that the prophet was there to anoint a king. He knew that his seven older brothers were brought in as candidates, while he was left out in the field with the sheep. A lesser, more insecure person would have been crying and bellyaching. They would have said, "God, I didn't even get a chance!"

We don't know exactly what David was doing, but there's no indication in the Word that he was whining, griping, or complaining. In fact, if he had done that, God would never have selected him anyway. Even though David was initially excluded, God passed by all the others and had them stand until he arrived. God considered, chose, and honored David, the one whom no one else considered. God looked on David's heart. He passed over everyone else to find David!

Lessons from David:

*For the eyes of the LORD run to and fro throughout the whole
earth, to show himself strong in the behalf of them whose heart
is perfect toward him.*

2 Chronicles 16:9

The word "perfect" in this verse doesn't mean sinless or
problem free. It means someone whose heart is fully committed,
completely belonging to the Lord; someone who is seeking God
with their whole heart. God passed over an entire nation, seven
older brothers—everybody—to find David. Then He made them
stand until David came. The Lord put honor, favor, and blessing
upon David because David had put honor, favor, and blessing upon
the Lord.

"Here I Am!"

God wants to do the same for you. You don't have to be a
silver vessel, just a surrendered one. It's not your ability; it's your
availability God is interested in. God is looking for someone who
will make Him first in their life. Your response to the Lord right
now ought to be, "Look no further! Here I am! I'm turning my life
over to You with my whole heart." If you will genuinely do that,
you'll be promoted. You'll see God's blessing come to pass in your
life.

The Bible describes David's appearance as "ruddy" (1 Samuel
16:12). This word literally means "red." Scholars aren't sure whether
this means that David was redheaded or just had a red complexion.
Either way, such an appearance would certainly be unusual for a Jew.

The word "ruddy" also has the connotation that he was pampered, what we would call a "Mama's Boy" today. He was also…

Withal of a beautiful countenance, and goodly to look to.

1 Samuel 16:12

These aren't necessarily bad traits or characteristics, but they aren't what you would expect in a warrior-king. It certainly wasn't what Samuel was expecting at the beginning. But God told him, "Don't look on the outward appearance. Look on his heart." God chose David, despite the fact that in the natural he didn't have the height, stature, build, or looks one would expect of a king. God chose him because of his heart.

Regardless of what your limitations are in the natural, God looks at your heart. Even if your body is handicapped, God isn't looking at that. He's looking at your heart. Your heart isn't handicapped unless you choose to let it be that way. You can choose God. You can seek Him with a perfect heart. And if you do, He'll raise you up and do miracles in your life just as He did for David.

Be Like David

Then Samuel took the horn of oil, and anointed him in the midst of his brethren: and the spirit of the LORD came upon David from that day forward. So Samuel rose up, and went to Ramah.

1 Samuel 16:13

Later in 1 Samuel 16, the Word goes on to say that David was chosen out of all the Israelites to come and play his harp before Saul because he was a valiant man and God was with him (1 Samuel 16:18). The one who recommended David to Saul was one of his servants. They were looking for someone who could play the harp and alleviate the torment Saul was experiencing from an evil spirit that was plaguing him. In the midst of this search, David's name just happened to be brought up. Coincidence? I don't think so!

Personally, I believe Samuel anointed David in secret because he was afraid of what Saul might do. But the principle is true: Once you have begun to seek the Lord and He releases His anointing on your life, you are like a cork. They could put you on the bottom of a lake, but you will still rise to the surface. It doesn't matter what they do. You're like cream—always rising to the top!

If you seek God with your whole heart, the eyes of the Lord will find you (2 Chronicles 16:9). He's looking for a person like that. He'll pass over everybody in your nation, state, and city just to find you. Once He locates you and releases His power into your life, He'll cause you to be drawn to the top. God will release His blessing through you into this world. It's just a matter of time. This is exactly what happened with David.

Don't be like Saul. He was a man pleaser, motivated by pride and arrogance. Since he was afraid of people, he was always trying to please them. This caused him to disobey God and say, "I'm not going to do it Your way. My way is better!" Saul refused to accept responsibility and became stubborn and rebellious instead. Humble yourself and accept responsibility. Come to the end of yourself and the beginning of God.

A Heart for God

Be like David. Prepare your heart to seek the Lord. He is not looking for people with talent, education, or natural abilities. He's not against such people, but neither is He for them. What God is looking for is a heart that seeks after Him. God chooses people based on their heart. If you hunger and thirst after righteousness, you will be filled (Matthew 5:6). You won't only be satisfied and have your needs met, but you'll also be filled with the power, presence, and provision of God. He will pour you out and make you a blessing to other people. Man looks on the outward appearance, but God looks on the heart.

Prepare Your Heart

If you are born again, God gave you a perfect heart. Quit walking in the vanity of your own wisdom and embrace the wisdom of God. Renew your mind to His Word so you can see yourself the way He sees you. Understand the riches He placed within your born-again spirit and how you can experience them day-by-day.

As a brother and fellow follower of God, I haven't yet arrived, but I have left. God has spoken these things into my life in a powerful way. I have prepared my heart to seek Him and be fully committed to Him. As you can tell, I'm not the most qualified person to do what I do. I'm a hick from Texas who dropped out of college after only six months. But the Lord has used me to raise up multiple Bible schools all around the world to train ministers and equip believers. In the natural, it doesn't make sense. But God saw my heart, not my education (or lack thereof). You can have thirty-two degrees and still be frozen!

Lessons from David:

I'm certainly not the best sounding or best looking person. Yet the Lord has me preach and teach His Word all around the world, both on radio and television. He could have easily chosen someone who sounded better, looked better, or dressed better. I really don't have a corner on anything in the natural. I have just sought the Lord with my whole heart and He has blessed me. He has used me, and I'm thrilled about that!

The Lord has a plan, a destiny, for you. As you seek Him with your whole heart, you'll find yourself walking in that plan more and more. I pray that you will let the Holy Spirit burn these truths into your heart so you will be a man (or woman) after God's heart too!

Chapter 6

Seeing Through the Covenant

David was anointed to be king in secret. Nobody knew he was king yet except his family and Samuel, and they were hiding it. If the present king, Saul, had heard this news, he would have killed them all. Samuel acknowledged this in 1 Samuel 16:2.

David had been playing the harp in the court of Saul, however Saul didn't know who David was. When the Philistines came down to fight, Saul went off to battle and sent David home. While he was home, David went back to keeping his father's sheep. A proud person wouldn't have been able to do this. David was the anointed and rightful king, but he was tending his father's sheep just like he had done before all this happened. Another characteristic of humility is patience, while impatience is a sure sign of arrogance and self-reliance.

Jesse's three oldest sons, Eliab, Shammah, and Abinadab, were in the army, so they went with Saul to battle. But as they went out to battle, a champion of the Philistines, a giant named Goliath, came out and challenged the armies of Israel.

Lessons from David:

The Philistine Champion

And there went out a champion out of the camp of the Philistines, named Goliath, of Gath, whose height was six cubits and a span.

1 Samuel 17:4

Most scholars believe that Goliath stood at least nine feet nine inches tall. Some even say he may have been as tall as thirteen feet!

And he had an helmet of brass upon his head, and he was armed with a coat of mail; and the weight of the coat was five thousand shekels of brass.

1 Samuel 17:5

Scholars estimate that the coat of mail that Goliath wore weighed about 125 pounds! The giant's armor alone probably weighed more than David!

And he had greaves of brass upon his legs, and a target of brass between his shoulders. And the staff of his spear was like a weaver's beam; and his spear's head weighed six hundred shekels of iron: and one bearing a shield went before him.

1 Samuel 17:6-7

These scholars also estimate that Goliath's spearhead weighed fifteen pounds. The actual shaft of his spear must have looked like a rounded off 4x4 post. It had to have quite a bit of weight in order to balance out the heavy spearhead. If the head was fifteen pounds and the shaft was another fifteen pounds to balance it out, then his spear weighed about thirty pounds. Can you imagine how hard it would be to throw a thirty-pound spear?

This is an indication of Goliath's size and strength. He wasn't tall and skinny. He was a well-proportioned, muscular giant of a man. In the natural realm, nobody could compete with him because he was easily their superior.

"What Is the Reward?"

And he stood and cried unto the armies of Israel, and said unto them, Why are ye come out to set your battle in array? am not I a Philistine, and ye servants to Saul? choose you a man for you, and let him come down to me. If he be able to fight with me, and to kill me, then will we be your servants: but if I prevail against him, and kill him, then shall ye be our servants, and serve us. And the Philistine said, I defy the armies of Israel this day; give me a man, that we may fight together. When Saul and all Israel heard those words of the Philistine, they were dismayed, and greatly afraid.

1 Samuel 17:8-11

The Israelites actually hid themselves behind rocks and in dens and caves. Among the entire nation of Israel, there wasn't a single person willing to go up against this giant Goliath.

David's father called him while he was keeping the sheep. He gave him some bread and cheese, and said, "Take this to your brothers and to the captain over them in the army. Find out how they're doing and bring me back word" (1 Samuel 17:17-18). Back then, they didn't have newspapers, radio, television, or Internet for news broadcasts. If you wanted to find out what was happening to your children who were out fighting in a battle, you had to send someone to get a first-hand report. So Jesse sent his youngest son David to do this.

As David arrived at the Israelite camp to see his brothers, the armies lined up as Goliath, this Philistine champion, issued his challenge once again. Then he cursed the Israelites and called them cowards as they fled from before him (1 Samuel 17:23-24). After David saw and heard these things, he asked, "What will be done for the man who kills this giant and takes away our reproach?" Instead of running away and being afraid like everybody else, David was saying, "This guy needs to be stopped! What are they promising the fellow who will go out and defeat this giant?"

The Right Way to Think

Remember, David was still a youth at this time. Most scholars believe he was around seventeen years old when he was anointed to be king. Therefore, he was probably eighteen or nineteen at the time he heard Goliath's challenge. He certainly wasn't very old. All of the seasoned men of war were bigger, stronger, and more experienced than David, yet they were standing around, full of fear. They were all shaking in their boots, but David challenged them saying, "What right does this man have to say these kinds of things?"

What made David able to fight this giant, kill him, and bring this great deliverance? He wasn't bigger or stronger than anyone else. It wasn't because he had been trained in a military school and had natural combat knowledge. It wasn't anything in the natural at all. The difference was David's heart—specifically the attitude of his heart. His heart was sensitive to God, therefore, he was fearless. He didn't see things the way other people saw them. They were looking on the outward appearance, but David knew that God looks on the heart. That's why he was chosen!

David not only saw himself the way God saw him, but he also viewed other things—including giants—the way God saw them. Goliath's heart was not right with God. He was not sensitive to the Lord at all. So in that sense, David already had him beat. It was an unfair fight, it really was. Goliath didn't stand a chance! Most people who consider outward appearances would have said, "David doesn't stand a chance. It's an unfair fight!" But when you look at the competitors from the inside, it was absolutely lopsided. David was the one who had the right heart, was anointed, and had the covenant relationship with God. Goliath had nothing. He was powerless. Now that's the right way to look at things!

What I'm saying here is different than the way most people think. That's why most people run and hide from their enemy behind rocks, in holes, and in caves. They don't think this way, but this is how the Bible will teach you to think. It's the right way to think!

Lessons from David:

A Word-Dominated Attitude

And David spake to the men that stood by him, saying, What shall be done to the man that killeth this Philistine, and taketh away the reproach from Israel? for who is this uncircumcised Philistine that he should defy the armies of the living God?

1 Samuel 17:26

David was expressing an attitude that was exactly opposite the rest of the Israelites. He was saying, "This guy is nothing. He's a nobody. He's easy!" Everyone else was saying, "He's so big and powerful! I'm nothing. I'm a nobody!" David had an entirely different attitude. Where did it come from? He stated it right here:

Who is this uncircumcised Philistine, that he should defy the armies of the living God?

1 Samuel 17:26

When David used this term "uncircumcised Philistine," he was saying that Goliath didn't have a covenant with God. Circumcision was a sign of the covenant God had made with the nation of Israel. He was saying, "We're superior. Why are we letting somebody who doesn't even have God on their side intimidate us?" David's attitude came from the covenant, the Word, and the promises of God.

Do you want a different attitude? Do you want to stand apart from all the people who are so fearful today? Those people are always griping, complaining, and talking about everything that could possibly go wrong. Do you desire to go out and make your life count? If you want to do exploits like David did, you need to have a different attitude. You have to look at God's Word and evaluate your enemy, circumstances, and problems based on what the Word says about them. David's confidence came from the fact that he had a covenant with God. He was dominated by what the Lord had to say, not what the physical presence of this giant or the army of Israel was saying. Only the Word—not other people—moved him. That's powerful!

Tremendous Opportunity for Victory

Even though I've seen this truth and lived it to a great degree, living in this physical world is like gravity. Unbelief, doubt, and negativity pull on us constantly. We need to be so dominated by God's Word that we do not let other people's opinions and what things look like in the physical realm dominate us. I have lived like this to a degree, but I desire to be stronger than ever before.

That's what made David different. He wasn't the strongest, biggest, meanest, or toughest. But David saw things differently than other people did. He looked at Goliath and said, "He's powerless. He doesn't have my covenant!" Nobody else had thought of the covenant or the promises of God. They were all just evaluating the situation based on Goliath's height, the size of his weapons, and the weight of his armor. They were only looking in the physical realm, but David was looking at the heart. Therefore, his conclusion was, *This man is bankrupt! He has nothing!*

It doesn't matter how big your problems are. If you would evaluate things as David did, you would recognize that you're the one with the promises. You're the one with an edge on any enemy you face. Really, the bigger the problem confronting you, the greater the opportunity you have to do an exploit for God, to see Him come through, and to have a better testimony. You'll be so blessed just knowing that you will get to see God deliver you from this totally impossible situation.

We never would have heard of David if he had killed a dwarf. Instead of praising him and talking about what a great battle it was, people would have criticized him and declared, "This was unfair!" The headlines in the morning paper would have read, "David Kills Dwarf: Sent to Prison for Life!" People would have criticized David if Goliath had been a dwarf, but the fact remains that he was a giant. This meant that David had a tremendous opportunity for the Lord to come through with an awesome victory. Therefore, instead of looking at how big our problems are, we should think of how great a testimony it will be when the Lord gives us victory over them.

Raised from the Dead

Even though facing the death of a child is a terrible thing and I wouldn't wish it on anyone, I've seen my son raised from the dead. When I first heard that he had died, I felt the same emotions anyone else would feel, but within a very short period of time I spoke my faith. Then I started thinking, *This is wonderful. What an opportunity this will be. I believe the Lord is going to raise him from the dead.* My son had been dead for approximately five hours, had turned black, and had already been toe tagged in the hospital cooler. Yet God raised him from the dead!

During the hour drive into town, before I knew what the outcome would be, I was excited, rejoicing, and praising God. You might think, "Come on Andrew, that's impossible! You couldn't have been rejoicing," but that is my testimony. I was there. I remember. That is how it was.

David was the same way. He wasn't intimidated. He knew he had a covenant with God. Due to this, David had a completely different attitude than most people. He thought, "What a great opportunity! I've been anointed king. This is what the Lord has called me to do—defend His people. So by His grace, I'm going to stand up and do it!"

This was what God used to propel David into the national public eye. Perhaps He could have done it some other way, we don't know. But this was how the Lord promoted David and got the entire nation to love him. After David killed Goliath, the women came out dancing and singing, "Saul hath slain his thousands, and David his ten thousands" (1 Samuel 18:7). David made the hit list! He was front-page news in all the papers. Beating Goliath actually paved the way for David to take over the kingdom of Israel. What an opportunity!

All the other fighting men were there, too. They had the same opportunity as David. They were Israelites—God's covenant people. They could have been used, but they weren't looking at the situation with Goliath through the covenant.

Lessons from David:

Speak Forth Your Faith!

David saw this opportunity through the covenant:

Who is this uncircumcised Philistine that he should defy the armies of the living God?

1 Samuel 17:26

David declared, "I have the Lord's promises, and this guy doesn't. He is separated from God. I have him licked, no problem!"

And when the words were heard which David spake, they rehearsed them before Saul: and he sent for him.

1 Samuel 17:31

David had to start speaking forth his faith. If he had just stood there and not spoken his vision, it wouldn't have come to pass. It wasn't enough for him to just boldly stand there while everyone else was running and hiding behind rocks, in caves, and such. He had to start speaking his faith. After he spoke those words of faith, the Lord promoted him. God took those words and passed them through the army, all the way up to the king.

You have to speak forth what the Lord has put in your heart. You can't be timid. Words are powerful. God will use your words to open up doors and stop the devil in his tracks.

Chapter 7

Overcoming Criticism

And Eliab his [David's] eldest brother heard when he spake unto the men; and Eliab's anger was kindled against David, and he said, Why camest thou down hither? and with whom hast thou left those few sheep in the wilderness? I know thy pride, and the naughtiness of thine heart; for thou art come down that thou mightest see the battle.

1 Samuel 17:28; brackets mine

David was standing up to the enemy, operating in faith, and doing nothing but good things that should be admired and praised. Yet when his older brother heard David's words, he railed on him. Eliab turned on David and began to question why he came, saying, "You're irresponsible. You've left those few sheep alone in the wilderness!" The truth was that David had not left the sheep alone. He left them with a keeper. Also, he didn't come down there on his own out of pride. David was submitting to his father, who had commanded him to go. David did everything *exactly* right.

Lessons from David:

Faith Condemns Mediocrity

If you're going to be a giant killer, you need to recognize that criticism will come your way. If you get a different attitude and start operating in faith instead of fear, if you stand up to your giants instead of running from them, if you recognize your covenant rights and privileges and start speaking forth your faith, you will be criticized. If you decide you aren't going to sit there and bow down to sickness, disease, poverty, oppression, and fear the way everyone else does, there will be people who will turn on you. They'll criticize your vision and mock you. It happens every single time.

When you believe for victory, speak forth your faith, and go for it, you condemn the average person's mediocre life. That's the number one reason they criticize and fight against you. If what you're saying about walking in health, prosperity, and joy is true, then they must be wrong. If you don't have to be defeated by circumstances, then their excuses are exposed. If you're saying, "It doesn't matter where you come from. All that matters is where you're going, because you can do all things through Christ," that confronts these people who have been saying, "Well, I'm a mess because of what my parents did when I was two years old. I was hated in the womb. I wasn't wanted. I'm a victim." Those who have been moaning, bellyaching, and using these things to excuse their ineffective, defeated, and powerless lives are going to be condemned by what you say. They have to do one of two things: repent and change, or criticize.

Either they will criticize, or they will say, "You know what, I've been wrong. I believed a lie. I can be prosperous, victorious, and healthy too. I'm changing, and I'm going to believe God's Word." Very few people do this because it requires integrity and taking responsibility for their attitudes and actions. Not many people are willing to do that. The average person will just try to discredit or stop you. Instead of climbing up to your level, they will just try to pull you down to theirs through criticism.

Anger and Jealousy

This was why David's oldest brother was so vicious toward him in saying these things. Eliab was there when David was chosen as the next king. The Word says David was anointed "in the midst of his brethren" (1 Samuel 16:13). And if you remember, Eliab was the first one the prophet Samuel looked at and rejected.

He looked on Eliab, and said, Surely the LORD's anointed is before him.

1 Samuel 16:6

When Samuel first saw Eliab, he became excited and thought that surely he must be the next king! This must have caused Eliab's hopes to soar. He must have thought, *I'm the oldest and strongest. I'm the toughest and meanest. Who would be king better than me?* Then he saw Samuel hear from God and pass over him—and all the others—in favor of the runt of the family. Eliab had to stand there along with all of his rejected brothers and honor David for however long it took for someone to go and fetch David. Eliab was angry and jealous. He must have wondered why God did not choose him.

Lessons from David:

When they were on the battlefield with Saul's army, Eliab had been hiding from Goliath just like all the other soldiers. He was operating in cowardice and fear. Then here came his little brother David, saying, "Who is this uncircumcised Philistine?" Boy, that must have gotten under his skin. It had to, because it forced him either to admit that his youngest brother was right, that David was a powerful man of God and he was a zero, or it would force Eliab to contend that he was right and David was not. In order for him to choose the latter, he would have to impute some kind of wrong to David.

Lawyers and Family

This happens all the time in court. When a person testifies and gives a condemning witness against someone else, nine out of ten times this is what the lawyer's tactic will be. They won't try to disprove what the witness is saying or defend their client. Instead, they will turn on the witness and try to discredit him. They will say, "This guy is a loser. He's been convicted of perjury. He's done this and that. He doesn't have any character." If they're successful in their efforts, the court will throw the witness' testimony out and all of the damage it could have done is reversed.

This happens on an individual basis, too. When you start talking victory saying, "God wants me well. I will prosper and succeed. No weapon formed against me will prosper," the person who is living a defeated life has to either repent or condemn you. The average person will condemn you, which is why criticism comes. If you get the attitude of David, if you start basing your evaluation of things on the covenant and get bold enough to speak it, you will be criticized. I guarantee it!

Many times this criticism comes through the people who know you the best, like your family. After Jesus' own brothers mocked him, He said:

A prophet is not without honour, but in his own country, and among his own kin, and in his own house.

Mark 6:4

The people who know you the best have a hard time believing there is really anything special about you because they know you. They know where you have been and what you have done. They know your mistakes and immaturity; everything about you. Since they are basing their judgment on outward appearances, it is hard for them to really see what God has done in you.

You'll Be Challenged

When I was first turned on to the Lord, some of my family were the very ones who said negative things toward me. They didn't do this maliciously. I've always loved my mother, brother, sister, and in-laws, and have enjoyed a pretty good relationship with them. But when I was first turned on to the Lord, I was fanatical! I started believing for miracles and confessing that I could receive the power of God. Some of my family members were critical of this—not because they hated me, but because they didn't understand it. When they looked at me, I was exactly the same as before. I was telling them that I'd had this special encounter with the Lord and He had spoken to me, but they weren't there. They didn't know what was going on because they were only looking on the outward appearance.

I'm not saying that all the criticism is mean and malicious, or that you can't overcome it. I'm just saying it's natural. The people who know you the best are still going to consider you as their little brother, neighbor, co-worker, or whatever. They don't know what God said, and they can't see what happened on the inside of you. But after a period of time they will understand. My family now basically embraces me and approves of what has happened. They know that something happened because it changed my life. Now they see me differently. However, prior to this, it was just my word. They didn't know everything because they couldn't see what had happened on the inside of me.

If you're going to become a giant killer, criticism will come. When you start trying to overcome your problems instead of just sitting down and being overcome by them, when you begin to believe and speak forth your faith instead of just running and hiding like everyone else, you'll be challenged. Criticism will come, and sometimes it will come from within your own family. But you just have to get on with it. You can't let criticism stop you. If criticism could kill you, I'd be dead!

Grasshopper or Giant Killer?

It doesn't matter what other people say about you. It's what you say about yourself that counts. This truth was clearly illustrated when Moses sent twelve men to spy out the Promised Land. Ten of them came back saying, "It's a good land, but we can't take it because there are giants there!"

We were in our own sight as grasshoppers, and so we were in their sight.

Numbers 13:33

Other people may criticize you because they don't see you the way God does. They aren't going to recognize your true power and potential. But it doesn't really matter what other people say. The opinions of others might be a factor, but it's not the determining factor. What really counts is how you see yourself. Do you see yourself as a grasshopper or a giant killer?

People have mocked, criticized, and railed on me over all kinds of things. They hadn't seen the power of God in my life and they didn't know what the Lord had spoken to me. But by the grace of God, I've been able to see differently than what people say. I know God has touched my life. I know He has done something on the inside of me. So it doesn't really matter what other people say about me. What matters is what I say about myself based on what God has spoken to me.

This is a tremendous lesson from the life of David. You need to find out who you are. You need to discover what God has called you to do. Then no matter what criticism you might face, go on in His power and do it!

Lessons from David:

Stay On Track

My good friend, Joe Nay, has made a huge impact on my life. He's the one who actually helped stir me up to seek the Lord. Immediately after I was turned on to Jesus, I started receiving criticism from both my family and my church. The leaders in my church would just rail on me. Due to my fanaticism, one of them wanted to excommunicate me, kick me out of the church. Even though I was still going on with God, all this criticism was beginning to wear on me. So I went to one of Joe Nay's meetings.

Joe called me out in front of everyone and started prophesying, "Andrew, I see you like a runner on a track. You're running a race and doing good, in fact you're out there leading the pack. But the people in the grandstands are criticizing you. They're yelling at you and telling you that you're doing it all wrong. I see you getting off of the track and going up into the grandstands to argue with the spectators. But even if you win the argument, you're going to lose the race. Don't worry about what other people say. Get back on track and finish the race. Do what God has told you to do!"

That was a powerful word that really ministered to me. I've even given it to other people in the form of a prophecy. If it worked for me, I believe it'll work for them. That's a powerful truth. God really spoke to me through that.

When you start going for it, Satan will raise up people to criticize you. His purpose is to divert you from doing what you're supposed to do. The devil wants to get you off track, get you arguing with spectators in the grandstands, justifying yourself to other

Overcoming Criticism

people, and trying to gain the approval of men. However, even if
you win the argument, you'll still lose the race. You need to get to
the place where you don't let criticism change you. Stay on track,
and don't let criticism change your message.

Who Cares?

This is exactly what David did. After his brother said all of
these things, he responded:

What have I now done? Is there not a cause?

1 Samuel 17:29

In other words, David said, "What are you on my case for? I
haven't done anything wrong!"

*And he turned from him toward another, and spake after the
same manner.*

1 Samuel 17:30

David just turned to the next guy and repeated the same words,
"Who is this uncircumcised Philistine?" He didn't let his older
brother's criticism slow him down one bit.

If you are going to be a giant killer, you're going to have to get
beyond criticism. If you're going to start overcoming problems and
bring deliverance to yourself and others, you're going to have to get
to where you aren't so touchy. Who cares what other people have
to say about you? David overcame this criticism and continued to
speak forth his faith.

Lessons from David:

And when the words were heard which David spake, they rehearsed them before Saul; and he sent for him. And David said to Saul, Let no man's heart fail because of him; thy servant will go and fight with this Philistine.

1 Samuel 17:31–32

Chapter 8

A Confident Testimony

And Saul said to David, Thou art not able to go against this Philistine to fight with him: for thou art but a youth, and he a man of war from his youth.

1 Samuel 17:33

After David received criticism from his own family, King Saul, the most powerful and influential man in the entire nation said, "You can't fight against this Philistine giant. You're just a youth, and he's a man of war. You don't stand a chance!"

David was bold because he believed God and was aware of his covenant. He recognized that this Philistine was uncircumcised and had no relationship with God. But even though David's faith was in the promises contained in God's Word, what he said next reveals where his confidence came from.

And David said unto Saul, Thy servant kept his father's sheep, and there came a lion, and a bear, and took a lamb out of the flock: and I went out after him, and smote him, and delivered it out of his mouth: and when he arose against me, I caught him by his beard, and smote him, and slew him. Thy servant slew both the lion and the bear: and this uncircumcised Philistine shall be as one of them, seeing he hath defied the armies of the living God. David said moreover, The LORD that delivered me out of the paw of the lion, and out of the paw of the bear, he will deliver me out of the hand of this Philistine.

1 Samuel 17:34-37

David was saying, "Look! I've already proven God to be faithful. I have a history! This isn't the first time I've ever believed God. I've trusted Him and seen Him work miracles through me before. Because of this past experience, I have confidence, hope, and I believe that it's going to happen again!"

Faithful in the Least

One of the reasons David was able to overcome the giant when the others couldn't was because he had been faithful and proven God in the small things.

Jesus said:

He that is faithful in that which is least is faithful also in much: and he that is unjust in the least is unjust also in much.

Luke 16:10

In other words, if you aren't faithful in a small thing, you won't be entrusted with the great things. Most people are waiting until they get into a crisis situation to believe God. However, they aren't trusting Him on a daily basis. They're taking the easy way out. Either they're learning to cope with things or they're not fighting for their God-given rights. They're taking a shortcut to get their needs met, but they aren't believing God.

In the area of health, some people plan to trust God if cancer ever knocks on their door. However, they pop a pill just as soon as they get a headache and they rely on medication to treat their colds. They take something to wake them up and something else to put them to sleep. They aren't trusting God for their health in the small things, but when the big thing comes like cancer, they think they're going to trust Him then. Right!

Don't misunderstand what I'm saying. God isn't mad at you if you take aspirin or cold medicine. I'm not saying you cannot take medication or that you're evil if you rely on those things. But I am asking: When are you going to start trusting God with your health? Are you waiting until something tragic happens and the doctors can't do anything about it, and only then will you begin to trust Him? If that's the way you're thinking, your faith isn't going to work.

The Growth Process

Your faith has to grow and increase with use. You do not go from zero to a thousand miles per hour in the Spirit instantly. You have to accelerate. You have to build up momentum and speed.

Jesus gave this illustration to help us understand the kingdom of God:

> *As if a man should cast seed into the ground; and should sleep, and rise night and day, and the seed should spring and grow up, he knoweth not how. For the earth bringeth forth fruit of*

herself; first the blade, then the ear, after that the full corn in the ear.

Mark 4:26-28

The kingdom of heaven works like a seed. You don't just plant an acorn and then—BOOM!—instantly it becomes a full-grown oak tree. It takes time and many seasons for the seed to go through the growth process to maturity.

First the blade, then the ear, after that the full corn in the ear.

Mark 4:28

This is a principle of God. It's how everything works. You don't just go from never having trusted God to all of a sudden killing a giant. You must start trusting the Lord in smaller things and then progress and increase.

A Big Vision

Once, I shared this truth with one of our Bible college students. This man had some problems. He had previously lived in a mental institution. He had been declared completely unable to work so he derived his total income from welfare. I really liked this guy. He was kind and had some great qualities, but he had never really trusted the Lord before in his finances.

As I ministered God's Word on prosperity and told the students they should be givers instead of takers, this guy really became excited. He came to me some time later and shared how he had found an old hotel, a historic building that was mostly stone.

It was a beautiful building, but it had burned awhile back and become derelict. It was water damaged, the roof was caved in, and in a number of ways, it was just structurally unsound. Anyway, the building was for sale for $1.5 million. This man talked to some builders and found out it would take between $2 million and $2.5 million to restore it. This would be a total of $4 million for both the purchase and restoration.

The man had it all worked out: how many rooms there were, what he could charge if he rented them all out, and other events he could host there to make money. He showed me on paper how he would pay off all of the loans, cover the expenses, and make a profit. It was a great idea. After telling me all of this, he asked, "What do you think about it?"

At first, I complimented him for the fact that he was breaking out of the poverty mentality and trying to believe God. I encouraged him and told him, "There are some really good things here, but I can guarantee you that this is not God. The Lord will not do this through you."

You might be thinking that I was terrible for discouraging him. I will admit, he was discouraged. In fact, he even became a little upset with me. But I told him that according to Mark 4, the kingdom of God works like a seed. There has to be a growth process! You can't go from never believing God for a quarter to make a phone call, right into raising $1.5 million. You can't jump from never having earned a dime in your entire life, to financing and pulling off a $2.5 million construction project. That's just not how the kingdom works.

Lessons from David:

Insignificant Matters

Sure enough, the man's plan didn't work out. Things didn't come together like he thought. But he's still growing and going on with God. Maybe sometime in the future, something will happen with that vision, but not right away. It's a growth process.

This battle between David and Goliath didn't happen the way some people imagine it. David didn't just go out there and all of a sudden, this spirit of faith came upon him enabling him to rise up and kill this giant. No, David had been seeking God. He had been faithful in smaller things.

In fact, David had been faithful in seemingly insignificant things. We don't know exactly how many sheep David kept, but according to Eliab's statement, it was just a few (1 Samuel 17:28). No matter what size the herd really was, in some ways it was insignificant. The herd certainly wasn't worth David's life. Even though shepherds were expected to defend the sheep by attempting to scare off wild animals, surely Jesse wouldn't have wanted David to die trying to save one lamb from a lion or a bear. He might have expected David to try to shoo the predators off doing things that are prudent, but certainly he did not expect his young son to go up and grab a lion or a bear by the beard, but that is exactly what David did (1 Samuel 17:35). No father would want his son to risk his life to save a sheep. Sheep are important, but not that important.

So basically, David had a very small responsibility. He wasn't tending a huge herd of sheep. In most people's opinion, the job definitely wasn't worth risking his life over. It was small, insignificant.

But David was faithful, even to the point of laying his life on the line in a small, insignificant matter.

Trust God Every Day

This is how you become a giant killer. You don't wait until big things like cancer knock on your door. You start trusting God in the small things every day. You fight to keep your joy and peace, as if you are fighting a giant out there. You stand on principle on the small things, doing what's right, even when nobody else is watching.

David was on the backside of the desert as he tended sheep. The grandstands weren't full. Nobody even knew what was going on. David may or may not have told other people what had happened when he fought the lion and the bear. This certainly wasn't something that hit the front pages of the local newspaper. David risked his life in a relatively insignificant matter, in a way that he might never have received recognition and acclaim for. Yet he was just as faithful with that as if it were something big and important.

Many people want the great victory, but few are willing to pay the price of faithfulness. Everybody wants to kill a giant and hear the people sing their praise, but very few are willing to risk their lives on the backside of the desert when nobody is watching. If you aren't faithful in small things, you won't be ruler over much. If you haven't started trusting God for the ability to overcome headaches and colds, chances are you won't be able to stand against cancer when it comes your way.

You need to learn to trust God in the everyday things. Do

you control your temper when somebody cuts you off in traffic? Or are you someone who gets upset, lays on the horn, and flashes them—God forbid—an obscene sign? If you can't control yourself with something small like that, you'll never make it when the big things come. If you aren't faithfully working for your boss, you'll never become the boss.

Why should God give you a better car if you aren't even taking care of the junk heap you have now? Is your car so full of food and trash that it's hard for somebody else to get in? Why would the Lord give you a new car to mess up? You might say, "Come on Andrew, you're straining at a gnat here. This isn't that important!" It may not be to you, but that's probably the reason why you haven't seen the mighty exploits yet. That very attitude may be why God hasn't used you in a bigger way.

Incremental Steps

One of the common traits I've noticed among people whom God is using in a mighty way is that they are faithful in the little things as well as the big. Even if there are only five people in attendance, they preach their heart out as if there were a thousand. They give it everything they've got. They're people of integrity who are faithful in the little things. They aren't just faithful when big things are on the line and someone's watching. They do the right thing even if nobody's looking.

This is one of the reasons God used David to kill Goliath. David was faithful in small things. He faithfully served his father and protected the sheep. This gave David confidence to fight the big battle.

The Lord recently told me that I was limiting Him in some ways and I needed to grow. So we moved from a 15,000 square foot building into an 110,000 square foot building, which was a giant step of faith for me. I went from zero payments to having a monthly building payment of $25,000. Our utility bill was also about $8,000 per month.

Then we outgrew that building and I started a 220,000 square foot building project for our new Charis Bible College campus, which will cost $52 million. We are building it debt free. But that's not the end. There is more to come. We couldn't have done this all at once. I've been growing in trusting the Lord for decades. I definitely couldn't have done these things without trusting God through the years, taking many incremental steps of faith along the way.

I remember when Jamie and I wrote out our first covenant. We were believing God for $300 per month. That $300 was the total income for both the ministry and us, and it allowed us to give $100 away each month. That's 33 percent. But I didn't get to that point of faith overnight. It took me a while to grow up to that.

When we moved to Manitou Springs and began our ministry in the Colorado Springs area, we had to believe God for about $700 per month to run the whole ministry, which we did. If I hadn't taken these incremental steps through the years, there's no way I could have believed God for $500,000 a month in 2003. This paid for my staff, building, equipment, radio and television bills, and other expenses. In 2013, our budget was $3 million per month, and this amount will only increase in the future. I couldn't do this had I not been faithful and believed God for those smaller things.

This is a tremendous principle that you need to grab hold of. You can't prepare any better for the future than by just starting to be faithful today. Make a decision today that you are going to start believing God, walking in joy, choosing to do the right thing, controlling your emotions, studying the Word, and blessing other people. Choose to spend time with God, even if there's nothing pressing. Just do it to be a faithful servant. Faithfully serve other people. Serve your boss today. Do things with integrity and excellence. If you do this over a period of time and prove yourself faithful, then when the giant comes knocking on your door, you'll have the ability to stand against him and overcome.

"The Kingdom Is in Your Hands"

Right after David testified to Saul about killing the lion and the bear, he boldly declared, "This uncircumcised Philistine will be like one of them!"

And Saul said unto David, Go, and the LORD be with thee.

1 Samuel 17:37

This was nearly as big a miracle as David killing Goliath. The terms of this contest had already been set forth. If Goliath won, all the Israelites would become the Philistines' servants. But if an Israelite won, all the Philistines would serve the Israelites. So when Saul said, "Go," he was basically putting his entire kingdom, the whole nation of Israel, into the hands of this youth whom he had just moments before told, "You don't stand a chance!"

Apparently, David's response to Saul's previous comments persuaded him that David did stand a chance against the giant. David spoke with such conviction conerning Gods faithfulness when he was faced with both the lion and the bear. He testified of how the Lord had proven Himself and come through for him again and again. There was so much authority and anointing on David's words that it literally caused the king to place his entire kingdom into his hands. Now that's a miracle!

I think Saul recognized the anointing of God on David's life. Saul had experienced this in his early years. He became a new man (1 Samuel 10:9) and was able to win some impossible battles (1 Samuel 11). I believe Saul was not only putting his faith in David, but also in the power of God that was on David's life.

Believe the Word You Speak

As you mature, people will respond to you. As you recognize your covenant and believe God, as you stand up and speak forth your faith, as you are faithful in the small things and grow, you'll come to a place where what you say will command respect. When you have absolute faith and confidence in what you're saying, it will inspire faith and confidence in those who hear you. When you know what you're talking about because of revelation and experience, not just theory, people will respond to you in ways they don't respond to others.

Lessons from David:

When I minister God's Word, I speak from my heart. I'm not just rehearsing something I've heard someone else say. I share what the Lord has shown me on whatever subject it is. In fact, I've never heard anyone preach the things we've discussed thus far in this book. These are things I've lived. They're coming out of the lessons God has personally taught me through the life of David.

People can perceive when you're ministering God's Word from your heart. It rings true and gives you credibility in their sight. That's when they will respond to you. If God has called you to be a leader, you need to apply these truths and become totally convinced of what He's given you to share. People have come up to me and remarked, "What you say is so convincing. It sounds so strong and overwhelming." That's because I am convinced. I believe the Word I teach, with all of my heart. When you believe what you speak with all of your heart, then the people who listen to you will be able to believe it with all of their heart too. That's a great lesson from the life of David.

Chapter 9

The Power of God

And Saul armed David with his armour, and he put an helmet of brass upon his head; also he armed him with a coat of mail. And David girded his sword upon his armour, and he assayed to go; for he had not proved it. And David said unto Saul, I cannot go with these; for I have not proved them. And David put them off him.

1 Samuel 17:38-39

At first, nobody believed in David. They judged him based on his external appearance. People stacked up his physical stature against Goliath's so they didn't believe in him. Finally, David spoke with such conviction, authority, faith, and power that he won the people over—including the king. They finally said, "Well, okay. Go! We'll trust you."

They wanted to arm David with Saul's armor. Saul was the largest, tallest, biggest, and strongest of all the Israelites. He had all of this armor and weaponry, yet he was still hiding. He had never fought Goliath. If Saul's armor wasn't going to grant him victory, what made him think it would give David victory?

Can you imagine David putting on Saul's armor? Here's this

little runt of a guy, swallowed up in the armor of the largest man in the entire nation of Israel. David could probably turn around in the armor without ever moving it. This armor was burdensome to him. David had enough wisdom to recognize that this wasn't the way it was going to work. He said, "I can't do this." It's not that the armor itself was evil, but David was trusting in the Lord. The issue was that David had never proved the armor. He wasn't familiar with it. It wasn't what he had used before. He wasn't trusting in some physical thing to overcome Goliath. His confidence wasn't in the protection the armor could give him. David knew it was his faith in God that would put him over. So he had enough sense to refuse to go into battle with something that had never worked for him before.

Stick with What Works!

People will try to talk you out of serving God. They'll say, "You're fanatical. You can't do it." But if you persist, they will finally say, "Well, okay. Do it. But at least do this." And they will then try to give you their theories about how it should be done. But their theories aren't working for them. They aren't doing anything. There's no victory in their lives, yet they're quick to tell you what to do. "Here, put on my armor that isn't working for me!"

God may have spoken something to you and you may be trying to obey Him. You are taking a step of faith, but the truth is that you aren't going with what's in your heart. You aren't doing what God told you to do. You're trying to live off of somebody else's revelation. They may mean well, but you can't go by what God has told someone else to do. You can't just attend some seminar and figure out how another person grew a church or business and then go back and do it that way, thinking if it worked for one, it'll work for another. You need to hear what God is telling you. You can't just be parroting things. You need to get in the presence of God and develop your own relationship with Him. Don't just take what He gave someone else. Hear for yourself what the Lord tells you to do, then go with it!

Andrew Wommack Ministries has given away millions of cassette tapes, not to mention CDs, books, DVD's and audio message downloads (most of my teaching series are available free as MP3 files at our website). That's no gimmick! The majority of the people who contact our ministry never give us a dime. Yet we send them CD's, DVD's, books, and other things. How does that work? It's the blessing of God!

There was a time in my life when I couldn't buy the Word. My wife had gone two weeks without food. She was eight months pregnant, and we were struggling. I looked at a man's tape table and knew that there were truths on those cassettes that could have changed my life and brought us out of poverty, but I couldn't buy them. My wife had tears in her eyes, and I was about to cry myself. It was a terrible situation. As I stood there, I made a promise. "Lord, if You ever show me something from Your Word that will help another person, I'll never deny them access to it because of finances." And I try to keep that promise.

If we have an entire series of messages, of course we suggest a donation. However, we give it to people regardless of what they can send. If it's something like twenty or thirty messages in a set, we'll make the tapes or CDs available to people one at a time, if they will get them that way. We don't want to hand out tens of thousands of tapes to people who aren't giving anything, but I try to make my messages available as much as I can. This has worked for me. I have faith for it.

Yet, I've had well known, international ministers come to me and say, "You're wrong! You need to sell your tapes. You could make a lot more money!" I'm not against other people selling their messages. They can do whatever they want. I don't think someone isn't trusting God or that they're a bad minister if they don't give their materials away. I'm just saying that this is what has worked for me—and I'm sticking with what works!

David's Strength

You need to become secure in the Lord and hear from Him. You need to have God tell you some things. Then, when He tells you something, don't let other people talk you out of it. Don't reason it away by saying, "Well, here's what God says, but it doesn't make sense. So I think I'll go ahead and do it this other way." You're getting off onto thin ice when you start doing something like that. You need to follow God and do what He says. That's where your strength lies.

David's strength wasn't in armor or a sword. It was in trusting God. When Goliath saw him walk out toward him with just a slingshot, he laughed at him. The giant disdained and even cursed him for coming out against him with sticks and stones. Goliath didn't recognize the power of God.

The Power of God

And he [David] took his staff in his hand, and chose him five smooth stones out of the brook, and put them in a shepherd's bag which he had, even in a scrip; and his sling was in his hand: and he drew near to the Philistine.

And the Philistine came on and drew near unto David; and the man that bare the shield went before him. And when the Philistine looked about, and saw David, he disdained him: for he was but a youth, and ruddy, and of a fair countenance. And the Philistine said unto David, Am I a dog, that thou comest to me with staves? And the Philistine cursed David by his gods. And the Philistine said to David, Come to me, and I will give thy flesh unto the fowls of the air, and to the beasts of the field.

Then said David to the Philistine, Thou comest to me with a sword, and with a spear, and with a shield: but I come to thee in the name of the LORD of hosts, the God of the armies of Israel, whom thou hast defied. This day will the LORD deliver thee into mine hand; and I will smite thee, and take thine head from thee; and I will give the carcases of the host of the Philistines this day unto the fowls of the air, and to the wild beasts of the earth; that all the earth may know that there is a God in Israel. And all this assembly shall know that the LORD saveth not with sword and spear: for the battle is the LORD's, and he will give you into our hands.

1 Samuel 17:40-47; brackets mine

This is tremendous! Goliath began to rail on and ridicule David.

Lessons from David:

He pointed out his physical weakness, comparatively small size, and lack of a sword. Then he cursed David by his gods. However, neither Goliath, nor Saul, nor the rest of the army knew that David wasn't just a youth. He was an anointed king. He had the power and anointing of Almighty God on the inside of him.

You're the Winner!

You can't always see that just by looking at someone. But the truth is that if you're born again, you have a covenant with God, and you're the winner. You're the one who is an anointed priest and king (Revelation 1:6; 5:10). Don't just approach your giant and listen to the railing diatribe they hurl against you. Instead, listen to what God has to say about you. "You're the winner. You're the one with authority. You're an anointed king!"

David was a king. Goliath didn't know it. Saul didn't know it. But David knew it. He knew he was anointed. So instead of responding to this curse and being intimidated, he came right back saying, "Your confidence is in your physical size, your sword, and your shield. But my confidence is in the name of the Lord. It's God who is going to fight for me. It's His battle today, and I'm going to take your head off of you!" David didn't even have a sword, yet he prophesied that he would behead Goliath.

David had thought this thing through. He didn't just see himself going out there and killing Goliath with a sling. He saw himself using a sword to cut his head off. David declared, "I'm going to lift your head off of you today and give the carcasses of all the

Philistines to the fowls of the air and the beasts of the field!" Then he ran at Goliath.

And David put his hand in his bag, and took thence a stone, and slang it, and smote the Philistine in his forehead: that the stone sunk into his forehead; and he fell upon his face to the earth. So David prevailed over the Philistine with a sling and with a stone, and smote the Philistine, and slew him; but there was no sword in the hand of David.

1 Samuel 17:49-50

David may have been a perfect marksman with his sling, or perhaps he may have just been good or even average. It's possible that he just went out there and slung that stone and God supernaturally directed it and caused it to hit its mark.

Little Is Much

I don't always do things perfectly, yet God takes those things and makes them work. I do what I can, and God adds His power and anointing to it.

Little is much when God is in it. Remember the story about the little boy who only had five loaves and two fish? (Matthew 14:16-18.) He barely had enough for his own lunch, let alone enough to feed the multitude. Yet when he gave it to Jesus, it multiplied, fed the multitude, and they had more left over after they were all full than when they began. That's what happens when you give God the little bit you have—He takes it and multiplies it to abundantly meet the need!

Lessons from David:

I believe that's what happened with David. He may have been good or even average with his sling, but it wasn't his marksmanship that killed Goliath. It was his trust in God. David went out there and slung that stone in faith. The Lord took what he had—a stone—and made it hit the mark! Notice that the Word says he...

Slew him; but there was no sword in the hand of David.

1 Samuel 17:50

Head Held High

Therefore David ran, and stood upon the Philistine, and took his sword, and drew it out of the sheath thereof, and slew him, and cut off his head therewith. And when the Philistines saw their champion was dead, they fled.

1 Samuel 17:51

David didn't stop once Goliath was down. He got on top of him, took his own sword out, cut off his head, and then held it up for everyone to see. Once the Philistines saw that Goliath was dead, they fled.

The Philistines didn't flee when they saw Goliath fall. They wondered if perhaps he was just wounded and could have gotten back into the fight. They thought that Goliath still might overcome and defeat David. Maybe they thought Goliath just fell, after all, big people sometimes have trouble lifting their feet or even trip over them. The Philistines who were watching this weren't sure that Goliath was dead. But once David stood on top of him, took Goliath's own sword out, cut off his head, and held it up, nobody doubted any longer whether Goliath would get up and fight again. This proved he was dead.

David didn't just fight his enemy and knock him down. He completely conquered and totally vanquished him! David made sure there was no way Goliath would ever get up and fight again. And once he held Goliath's head up, all the Philistines fled. That's when deliverance came. That's when the Israelites began to chase the Philistines and win this battle!

Many times we resist the devil and fight just enough to get some relief. We knock him *down,* but we don't knock him *out.* Therefore he rises up and fights us again another day. It's like chasing your enemy over the hill until they are out of sight. Since you're out of immediate danger, you don't pursue him. You let him go. You allow him to regroup and come back to fight you again.

David didn't do that. He didn't just knock Goliath down. David fought his enemy until he was destroyed. He was taking no prisoners. He was literally out to destroy the enemy.

Finish the Job!

In 1991, the United States, Britain, and the coalition forces came against Saddam Hussein's regime in Iraq. They had him on the ropes, but they backed down. Instead of just walking into Baghdad and finishing the job, they pulled out.

There appears to be strong evidence suggesting that Iraq financed terrorists. So it's possible that if the U.S. and its allies would have finished the job in 1991, there never would have been the terrorist attacks on September 11, 2001. There wouldn't have been airplanes crashing into the World Trade Center and the Pentagon, and that airplane that seemed to be heading for the White House would never have crashed in a field. There wouldn't have been all the loss of life or the need for a second war with Iraq in 2003.

But the United States and its allies accomplished their initial objective and the immediate pressure was relieved. They had humiliated Saddam Hussein and his people. They thought that was enough. They didn't pursue their enemy until he was destroyed. Because of that, they had to come back twelve years later and do it again at the cost of many lives, money, resources, world opinion, and a lot of other things that could have been saved had they just taken care of finishing the enemy the first time.

Don't just resist the devil until you get some relief. Fight him until his work is totally destroyed. If you have arthritis, don't just pray and say, "Well, it's decreased. I can live with it now." No! Fight that thing until there's not a trace of it left. Don't just sit there and say, "Well, I was in absolute poverty. I believed God and now we're okay. We aren't really getting along the way we should, and I certainly can't give the way I'd like to, but we're okay. I think I'll just settle here." No! That's not the right attitude. You need to fight poverty until you destroy it. Keep believing God until you come out on top and truly abound so much that you can give into every good work like it says in 2 Corinthians 9:8. Don't settle for just enough for you. Pursue the manifestation of prosperity to the point that you can become a blessing to others..

You need to pursue the blessings of God and defeat your enemy until he cannot rise again. You need to get the attitude that you are taking no prisoners and giving no quarter. You are going to fight the devil and destroy him. You need to get this attitude.

Fight Now or Fight Later

Once you cut the head off of the problem you're fighting and hold it up for all to see, all the other demons will begin to flee. When the Philistines saw David hold up the head of their champion, Goliath, they fled. But they didn't flee until they were certain Goliath wasn't going to get back up again. Once the enemy sees that you have this attitude that you are going to totally vanquish him from your life, that's when he and all the other demons will flee.

The only reason the devil fights us so hard is because he's a coward. He knows that if he doesn't fight you now, he'll have to fight you later. So he'll fight you if he thinks he can get you to back down and cower before him. But once he sees that you're going to take it to him, he will tuck his tail and run!

David didn't overcome Goliath because of anything natural. It wasn't his talents, skills, looks, or charisma. In the physical realm, he was inadequate in every way. But on the inside, David was a man after God's own heart. He trusted and believed God. He had proven the Lord's promises before and had been faithful in the small things. David stood on what had worked for him. He wasn't going to go with someone else's plan. He did what God had shown him to do and pursued the devil until he literally destroyed him. If you get these attitudes and live them out over a period of time, you'll become a giant killer too!

Lessons from David:

Chapter 10

Encourage Yourself in the Lord

D avid was driven from the land of Israel right before he became king because Saul was hotly pursuing him. He moved into the land of the Philistines and was living among them (1 Samuel 27:1-3). He gained favor with Achish, the Philistine king of Gath. Gath is the same place Goliath was from. Achish gave David the city of Ziklag to dwell in (1 Samuel 27:5-6), however when the Philistines were marshaling their forces to go to battle, the princes didn't trust David to go with them so he and his men were sent home. When they returned, they saw that the city had been invaded by the Amalekites. They must have known that the city was unprotected.

> *So David and his men came to the city, and, behold, it was*
> *burned with fire; and their wives, and their sons, and their*
> *daughters, were taken captives. Then David and the people*
> *that were with him lifted up their voice and wept, until they*
> *had no more power to weep.*
>
> *1 Samuel 30:3-4*

This was a terrible situation! Can you imagine experiencing

something so tragic that you wept until you couldn't weep anymore? I've done that. The Scripture also says that the Amalekites had plundered the city and taken spoils (1 Samuel 30:19). David was experiencing a devastating loss and this was on top of thirteen years of being persecuted, chased, threatened, ridiculed, falsely accused, and thought of as crazy!

Get a picture of this: David was about seventeen years old when Samuel anointed him to be king. This instance in 1 Samuel 30:1-4 takes place just a day or two shy of when he actually began his reign at the age of thirty (2 Samuel 5:4). He'd operated in integrity and faithfulness but at the same time, had experienced troubles day in and day out for about thirteen years. He'd experienced problem after problem. Things never got better, only worse. David couldn't even go home to his people in Israel, but instead had to live among a people that had been his enemy. And on top of all that, now all of his wives and children had been taken and the city in which he lived had been burned to the ground.

David, however, wasn't the only one who had been through distress and suffered loss; all of his men had been with him. The Scripture goes on to say:

And David was greatly distressed; for the people spake of stoning him, because the soul of all the people was grieved, every man for his sons and for his daughters.

1 Samuel 30:6

This just adds insult to injury! The guys who had been with David through all his troubles turned on him, as if it was his fault all of these things had happened! He had provided for them, led them to victory in battle, and how did they repay him? They blamed him for this tragedy! David could have just quit right here. Most people wouldn't have survived this one incident, let alone what David had been through the previous thirteen years. Yet, this was happening less than twenty-four to forty-eight hours from David seeing his dreams fulfilled.

David Was No Fool

If David had quit and given up, which is what he was tempted to do, he wouldn't have become king. He could have given up and his men would have dispersed, or he could have said, "What's the use? What's the point in living now?" and let his men kill him. This is just like what Job's wife told him after they had been through terrible loss:

Dost thou still retain thine integrity? curse God, and die.

Job 2:9

There's a great lesson in this. I guarantee you will be pushed to a place where you will think, "Why even try anymore? I should just give up." But look at how Job answered his wife when she made that suggestion:

Thou speakest as one of the foolish women speaketh.

Job 2:10

It would have been foolish for David to give up, even in the face of this tragic situation. But David was no fool! He stuck with

Lessons from David:

God no matter what. The Bible tells us how he responded:

But David encouraged himself in the LORD his God.

1 Samuel 30:6

This is powerful! I can't tell you how many times God has used this to speak to me. I've been in situations where in the natural, it looked like I ought to just quit. Then I remembered this passage of Scripture and realized that David was in a worse place than I have ever been in, yet he was able to encourage himself in the Lord. Very few people do this. They're always calling somebody else, depending on them to bring encouragement. But you have to get to where you encourage yourself in the Lord. How do you do that? There are lots of ways to do this. Right here in the very next verse, it says,

And David said to Abiathar the priest, Ahimelech's son, I pray thee, bring me hither the ephod. And Abiathar brought thither the ephod to David.

1 Samuel 30:7

The ephod was a breastplate that the priests wore and somehow or another, God could communicate through the stones that were on it. This would be comparable in our day to the Word of God. God speaks to us through the Word. David encouraged himself by going back to the Word. I've done this same thing many times. I just go to the Word, start remembering the promises God gave me, and encourage myself in Him.

Speak in Tongues

Another benefit that I think a lot of Christians do not take advantage of is speaking in tongues. The Scripture says in 1 Corinthians 14:

He that speaketh in an unknown tongue edifieth himself.

1 Corinthians 14:4

The word "edify" means to build up. It says something similar in Jude:

But ye, beloved, building up yourselves on your most holy faith, praying in the Holy Ghost.

Jude 20

That's talking about speaking in tongues too. When you speak in tongues, you are building yourself up on your most holy faith. Now, I know there are a lot of people who don't understand these verses and they say, "What does speaking in tongues have to do with anything? It's total gibberish! I don't see how speaking in tongues would make a difference." But one of the very reasons that speaking in tongues is so powerful is because it doesn't make sense to the natural mind.

If therefore the whole church be come together into one place, and all speak with tongues, and there come in those that are unlearned, or unbelievers, will they not say that ye are mad?

1 Corinthians 14:23

Your carnal mind will say you're foolish for speaking in tongues.

It will try to stop you. But the reason speaking in tongues is so powerful is because if you do it over a prolonged period of time, it forces you to get into your most holy faith. Why? Because you don't know what you're saying.

> *For he that speaketh in an unknown tongue speaketh not unto men, but unto God: for no man understandeth him; howbeit in the spirit he speaketh mysteries.*
>
> *1 Corinthians 14:2*

When it comes to speaking in tongues, there's a tendency not to do it. It takes faith to believe that there's actually a benefit to doing it. But as the Scriptures say in 1 Corinthians 14:4, you edify yourself when you speak in tongues. You are building yourself up and promoting your spiritual growth. In order to pray in tongues over a prolonged period of time, you have to move into faith because you have to overcome thoughts that what you're doing is silly and foolish. But if you persist, you'll move into faith and begin to edify yourself.

I say all this to say that for the New Testament believer, when you need encouragement like David did, you can pray in tongues and build yourself up. If you've been filled with the Spirit, this is a resource you need to use. It's with you all the time! God has given this resource to you, and you can speak in tongues anytime you want and receive this benefit. This is tremendous!

There are many Spirit-filled people who will allow themselves to go into depression. They will sit there and pray, "God, I need something. Would You please send someone my way?" I'm not denying the fact that God can use other people. I believe that God is using me right now to speak to you. If you've been praying for direction from God, here's help coming your way: You need to be like David and encourage yourself in the Lord. In the New Testament, speaking in tongues is one of the most important things that you could possibly do.

Hold On!

There's not a single a Christian who is facing something more than they can bear.

There hath no temptation taken you but such as is common to man: but God is faithful, who will not suffer you to be tempted above that ye are able; but will with the temptation also make a way to escape, that ye may be able to bear it.

1 Corinthians 10:13

Satan doesn't have different things to throw at you. It's the same contents with a different wrapper and a different bow on it. You will never have to endure something you just can't handle. You might think that's not true, that I don't know your situation. Well, I know the Word of God, and God promised He would not suffer you to be tempted above what you are able to handle. Everything you're facing is what's common to man. When it seems like you can't stand another minute and you've hit your limits, God is going to make some way of escape so you can survive and come through victoriously.

David was in that situation, but if he would have given in to his hurt and pain and just given up hope, he would have done so only hours before he would have received what he had been patiently waiting on for thirteen years. I'm telling you, if you feel like you should quit, you could be just moments away from seeing the breakthrough you've been looking for.

You've got to encourage yourself in the Lord and stand on the promise that He will not suffer you to be tempted above what you are able to handle. God is telling you to hold on! Don't quit! Don't give up! Encourage yourself in the Lord. God is going to come through.

After David encouraged himself, he asked God what he should do about his situation:

And David enquired at the LORD, saying, Shall I pursue after this troop? shall I overtake them? And he answered him, Pursue: for thou shalt surely overtake them, and without fail recover all.

1 Samuel 30:8

The rest of this story says that David took leadership of his men, they submitted unto him, and he pursued the Amalekites, caught them off guard, and completely destroyed them. This is a great example of what I was talking about in the previous chapter: David pursued his enemies until they couldn't come back. He didn't just fight the Amalekite army until he couldn't see them anymore; he kept going until he utterly destroyed them! We need to learn to do the same thing in our lives.

David and his men got back every woman, every child, and all of their livestock—they didn't lose a single life. Plus, they got all the spoil of the Amalekites! God blessed them. Then, just hours after this, David received the news that Saul had been killed in battle, and he was crowned king. So after thirteen years, when things were at their worst, David encouraged himself in the Lord and that's when he saw the breakthrough!

You might be contemplating quitting, but remember what Peter said:

Lord, to whom shall we go? thou hast the words of eternal life.

John 6:68

Where else can you go? Who else has the words of everlasting life? You don't have anywhere else to go; you just need to stand and believe God. You need to get to the place David was. His dreams began to come to pass in a relatively short period of time because he didn't quit. If you will stand your ground and encourage yourself in the Lord, you'll become a victor like David. You'll outlast what the devil is trying to do in your life. This is one of the great lessons you can learn from the life of David.

Lessons from David:

Chapter 11

Actions and the Heart

Let's contrast Saul, who was the first king of the nation of Israel; David, who has been the focus of our study; and Absalom, David's son who tried to take the kingdom from his father by force. These are the three kings we're going to look at.

David is one of the central figures of the Bible. Only Moses had more chapters written by him and about him. This means that by sheer volume, David occupies the attention of a tremendous amount of scripture. He's the only person the Word calls "a man after God's own heart" (1 Samuel 13:14).

Born-Again Spirit

As New Testament believers, every one of us who have been born again now have God's heart placed within us. This is a fulfillment of Ezekiel's prophecies:

Lessons from David:

And I will give them one heart, and I will put a new spirit within you; and I will take the stony heart out of their flesh, and will give them an heart of flesh.

Ezekiel 11:19

A new heart also will I give you, and a new spirit will I put within you: and I will take away the stony heart out of your flesh, and I will give you an heart of flesh. And I will put my spirit within you.

Ezekiel 36:26–27

Every born-again Christian has a recreated heart that is superior to what David had. However, not every believer operates in this. Even David himself, the man after God's own heart, didn't always operate in accordance with the Lord. He had flesh flashes that were devastating.

We're going to look at these three kings and give priority to showing that David walked in the superior way. This doesn't mean that everything he did was right. God's Word records his sins, too. But we need to look at these three kings in order to see what made David a man after God's own heart.

An Imperfect Relationship

In contrast to both Saul and Absalom, David's heart was what made him a man after God's own heart. It wasn't primarily his actions, but his heart.

When talking about what grants us God's favor—what things

the Lord looks at that please Him—most people today will put the emphasis on actions. The Word reveals, however, that there is a relationship between what's in our heart and our actions.

> *But wilt thou know, O vain man, that faith without works is dead? For as the body without the spirit is dead, so faith without works is dead also.*

> *James 2:20, 26*

The Bible calls a person a hypocrite who says they are something but whose actions never back up that description. So there is a relationship between actions and what is really in someone's heart. However, it isn't necessarily a perfect relationship.

Actions aren't always a perfect reflection of what's truly in a person's heart. For instance, David—a man after God's own heart—committed adultery and then murder in order to cover up his adultery. Now certainly, those weren't expressions of God's heart. When David did this, he was unplugged from the Lord. He wasn't walking with God. But even though David sinned in doing these things, he remained a man after God's own heart.

As you and I become people after God's own heart, it will be reflected in our actions. If someone claims to be something but there are no actions to back it up, then it's appropriate to call them hypocritical. However, we can have a good heart and still do some stupid things. We can have a heart after God and still have occasional flesh flashes where we do some severely wrong things.

Once David was reproved, the way he responded to his sin by both his attitude and actions, revealed God's heart. In our church world today, I think we're too judgmental of people's actions. We need to take them into account. We can't just separate a person from their actions, because actions are an indication of what's inside a person. But there's more to it than that. It's a heart issue.

Comparative Morality

There's no record in Scripture of Saul ever committing adultery. He was never reproved over sexual immorality of any kind. It's possible that there could have been some of this type of sin in his life, but if there was any, it wasn't an issue. And it certainly wasn't why God rejected him.

Before Absalom rebelled against David, there is no record in Scripture of him committing any sexual sin. As a matter of fact, he was quite offended by the rape of his sister Tamar, who was raped by their mutual half-brother Amnon. Absalom was so incensed over this that he took Tamar into his own house and raised her. He even had a daughter whom he named Tamar, apparently in honor of his sister. Ultimately, Absalom murdered Amnon for what he had done to Tamar. By the way Absalom responded to the sexual abuse of his sister, we can deduce that he certainly held high moral standards, at least in respect to treatment of his sister.

So out of these three kings—Saul, David, and Absalom—David is the only one recorded in Scripture as having committed adultery (though as part of Absalom's rebellion against his father, he did commit adultery with David's wives in public). David took another man's wife and then had her husband killed. So in a sense, Saul and Absalom were more moral than David in many ways.

That's a relative statement, however, because Saul killed all but one of the sons of a priest—eighty-five men in total (1 Samuel 22:11-21). That was out and out murder! These men were ministers. They were unarmed. Even though I disagree with his conclusion, Saul reasoned that they had committed treason. So you could look at Saul's actions as the rightful execution of a group of people who were plotting treason. This was not the case in actuality, but in Saul's deranged frame of mind brought on by his insecurities, I believe Saul justified it as such. What he did wasn't right, but it wasn't any worse than what David did when he had Uriah killed to try to cover up his sin with Bathsheba.

Absalom murdered his half-brother Amnon because he had raped his sister Tamar. Although this could be viewed as justice or revenge, it doesn't justify what Absalom did.

As far as actions are concerned, David wasn't any better than Saul or Absalom. Therefore, we can conclude that it's not just our actions that reveal whether or not we have a heart after God. It must go deeper than that.

Consider the Heart

What really set David apart was the attitude of his heart. Integrity begins with an attitude. It doesn't end with it, and that's not all there is to it, but it has to go that deep. David had failures just the same as Saul and Absalom. In some ways, his failures were even worse. But the Word still calls him a man after God's own heart.

Today we tend to judge people only by their actions without

looking beyond to their heart. Actions are important, but people are more than just physical bodies who act. There are emotional and spiritual parts on the inside of us that drive us to do things. We have to take that into account as well.

I've had certain employees who just had a bad attitude. Their hearts, not just their actions, were wrong. Because of that, they didn't give me a good day's work. They talked about me behind my back and sowed discord among the other employees. When I see behavior such as that, I'll consider their actions but I'll also go beyond and look at their heart. I'll ask, "Are they vindictive or malicious in doing this? Are they trying to hurt people, or is this just a mistake?" As a leader, I look at and deal with actions because the other employees are watching what's going on, but I try to take into account the person's heart.

I remember one employee in particular who was just as faithful as could be. Although I paid him for forty hours of work each week, he put in fifty or sixty hours and never charged me overtime. He was just a hard worker with a great attitude who for years was faithful, faithful, faithful.

Then he started doing some things that were wrong. At first I wondered what was going on, then after a while I had every right to go in and fire him, saying, "That's it! You did this, this, and that and I've already talked to you about it. You're fired!" But even though I had the right to do that, I knew his heart. I knew these actions were inconsistent with his past behavior and what I knew to be his heart.

"These Actions Are Inconsistent"

So instead of blasting him, I went in, sat down, and said, "You've done these things, but I know that's not you. What's going on? Why have you started doing these kinds of things? That's inconsistent with what I know to be your heart." Instead of reproving him, I complimented him and asked, "Is there something I can do to help you work through this? There must be something that's causing you to act this way."

He never did open up and tell me what was wrong, but he humbled himself and said, "You're absolutely right. I am not treating you right as an employer. You will not have another problem!" Although he didn't choose to open up and tell me what was going on, he repented and promised to straighten it out. He did, and I never had another problem from him! Later I found out he was having some serious problems at home that caused those actions. If another person had done the exact same things that he did, I might not have handled the situation the same way. If their heart was wrong and I knew it, I wouldn't be able to show them as much latitude. If I made them submit in these areas, then the problem would just show up again somewhere else because their heart was wrong. The Word says:

> *For as he thinketh in his heart, so is he.*
>
> *Proverbs 23:7*

If the actions belie a heart problem, I would just terminate the employee right then. But for someone with a good heart who is doing the wrong things, I deal with them differently.

Lessons from David:

Develop His Heart!

We are human beings, not machines or human "doings." We are more than just what we do. We're people who make mistakes. There is more to us than just our actions. This is why we're going to focus our attention on David's heart attitudes. If you want to be a person after God's own heart, you're going to have to get beyond just behavior modification and trying to fulfill a set of rules and regulations. You need to get a heart like God's. You need to develop characteristics in your heart that are like Him.

This won't guarantee that you'll never do anything wrong. David certainly did some things wrong. However, having this kind of heart will minimize the things you do wrong. And when God reproves you, having a heart like God's will cause you to quickly repent. You'll be able to regain your position and your effectiveness and go on, whereas other people who do not have a heart like God's will be destroyed by their wrong actions.

Chapter 12
"It's My Fault!"

D avid had a relationship with God on a heart level. There were qualities, characteristics, and attitudes in his heart that set him apart from Saul and Absalom.

In 1 Samuel 15, God told Saul through Samuel to execute judgment upon the Amalekites. These people had attacked and shown no mercy to the Israelites while they were wandering in the wilderness. Due to this, the Lord had determined their absolute destruction. Many years after this transgression, God through Samuel sent Saul on a mission to utterly destroy everything of the Amalekites including their men, women, children, cattle, sheep, oxen, everything they possessed. This wasn't a battle to get spoils or a conquest where they could acquire property; this was a battle to exact God's vengeance and punishment. Therefore God commanded Saul, "Wipe out everything that breathes!"

However, Saul didn't do that. He claimed to have obeyed God, but he didn't. He saved Agag, king of the Amalekites, and brought all of the best sheep, oxen, and cattle back with him. Samuel went to see Saul after this mission.

Lessons from David:

*And Samuel came to Saul: and Saul said unto him, Blessed
be thou of the LORD: I have performed the commandment of
the LORD. And Samuel said, What meaneth then this bleating
of the sheep in mine ears, and the lowing of the oxen which I
hear?*

1 Samuel 15:13-14

The command included killing *all* of the animals. Yet Samuel
could hear both sheep and oxen. Saul had not fully obeyed the
command.

Sacrifice?

*And Saul said, They have brought them from the Amalekites:
for the people spared the best of the sheep and of the oxen, to
sacrifice unto the LORD thy God; and the rest we have utterly
destroyed.*

1 Samuel 15:15

Saul claimed that he had performed everything the Lord had
told him to do, but Samuel reproved him by saying, "No, you didn't.
These animals are still alive." Then Saul answered, "The people
spared the best."

Picture this! Saul was the king. He had been given a command
to kill everything that breathed. Yet here he was, saying, "the people"
spared these. Who was the king? Who was in the position of
authority? Saul was. So the people couldn't have done this if Saul
had not allowed it. At the very least, Saul had to give his approval.
More likely, he was the instigator of it. However, Saul wasn't

accepting responsibility for what he had done. Instead, he pushed responsibility off onto the people.

Saul placed the blame on somebody else and then tried to whitewash it by saying, "Well, we might not have killed them the way you told us to, but we brought them back here so we could slaughter them as sacrifices. Instead of just killing them and letting their death be in vain, we wanted to bring them back and offer them to the Lord."

If—and that's a big "if"—what Saul was saying was truly what they meant to do, then they were planning to offer a sacrifice to the Lord that cost them nothing. Maybe they said, "Let's bring back some of the enemy's herds and offer them to God. Then we won't suffer a depletion of our own herds when we celebrate this victory. Besides, we're just going to kill them anyway." This is totally an ungodly way of doing things. David shows us why.

No Positive Spin

Later in life, David came to Araunah's threshing floor to offer a sacrifice to the Lord (2 Samuel 24:18-25). When David spoke to him about securing the location for sacrifice and animals to offer, Araunah said, "Here, take my oxen. Take my yokes and use them for fire. Take all of these things—I give them to you!"

But David answered, "No, I'm going to pay you for it."

Araunah continued, "No, I want to give them to you!"

Lessons from David:

And the king [David] said unto Araunah, Nay; but I will
surely buy it of thee at a price: neither will I offer burnt
offerings unto the LORD my God of that which doth cost me
nothing.

2 Samuel 24:24; brackets mine

What a great attitude! You can't take your neighbor's sheep and offer it as a sacrifice to God. If you aren't giving of yourself, of your own substance, if what you are offering isn't costing you anything, it really isn't a sacrifice.

If this was truly what motivated them to bring back the Amalekites' oxen and sheep, then they were trying to find a cheap way of fulfilling their duty to offer sacrifices to the Lord for His protection in battle. "Let's not offer our animals, but theirs for the sacrifice!" Even if this was what they truly intended to do, there was no way to whitewash their disobedience and put a positive spin on it.

The First Career Politician

Then Samuel said unto Saul, Stay, and I will tell thee what
the LORD hath said to me this night. And he said unto him,
Say on. And Samuel said, When thou wast little in thine own
sight, wast thou not made the head of the tribes of Israel, and
the LORD anointed thee king over Israel? And the LORD sent
thee on a journey, and said, Go and utterly destroy the sinners
the Amalekites, and fight against them until they be consumed.

Wherefore then didst thou not obey the voice of the LORD, but didst fly upon the spoil, and didst evil in the sight of the LORD?

And Saul said unto Samuel, Yea, I have obeyed the voice of the LORD, and have gone the way which the LORD sent me, and have brought Agag the king of Amalek, and have utterly destroyed the Amalekites. But the people took of the spoil, sheep and oxen, the chief of the things which should have been utterly destroyed.

1 Samuel 15:16-21

Saul acknowledged that he understood the command was to utterly destroy the Amalekites and all they possessed, and yet he didn't do it. So this wasn't a deception; it was a lie. He was putting his spin on things. Saul was the first real career politician. You could ask him a question, but the answer he gave always depended on which side of his mouth he spoke from. (Now that's not true of every politician, but certainly a large number of them.)

But the people took of the spoil, sheep and oxen, the chief of the things which should have been utterly destroyed, to sacrifice unto the LORD thy God in Gilgal.

And Samuel said, Hath the LORD as great delight in burnt offerings and sacrifices, as in obeying the voice of the LORD? Behold, to obey is better than sacrifice, and to hearken than the fat of rams. For rebellion is as the sin of witchcraft, and stubbornness is as iniquity and idolatry. Because thou hast rejected the word of the LORD, he hath also rejected thee from being king.

1 Samuel 15:21-23

The prophet reproved Saul for his disobedience.

"I'm Responsible!"

David also disobeyed the Lord. He committed adultery, murdered the woman's husband, and then took her as his wife in an attempt to cover up the adultery and make it look like the child that had been conceived was actually legally his by marriage. What David did was terribly wrong, but once he was reproved, he repented in sackcloth and ashes. He didn't point the finger at anyone else. David accepted the blame and took responsibility for his actions.

You can't commit adultery with just one person. Although Bathsheba was involved in this too, David never said anything like, "She enticed me. It's her fault. Bathsheba shouldn't have been washing herself up on the roof without her clothes on. She's the one who exposed herself to me!" Neither did he say, "Joab helped me kill Uriah." You don't find any of that in the Bible.

David wrote Psalm 51, a psalm of repentance for all he had done in this instance. The subscript to the psalm reads:

To the chief Musician, A Psalm of David, when Nathan the prophet came unto him, after he had gone in to Bath-sheba.

Verse 4 of the psalm really shows David's heart during this time:

"It's My Fault"

Against thee, thee only, have I sinned, and done this evil in thy sight: that thou mightest be justified when thou speakest, and be clear when thou judgest.

All through Psalm 51, David was saying, "God, it's my fault! I did this. I'm responsible." Whenever David sinned, he took responsibility for his actions by saying, "Lord, I'm the one who numbered the people. I'm the one who transgressed against You. But these sheep, what have they done?" (2 Samuel 24:17). David accepted responsibility.

Feeling Justified

Contrast this with Saul in 1 Samuel 15. Twice he said, "It's the people who did this. They made me do it!" He just wouldn't admit he was wrong. He refused to accept responsibility and kept pointing the finger at someone else.

Absalom also refused to own up to his sin. He simply would not acknowledge that his problems and his estrangement from his father, David, happened because he murdered his brother, Amnon (2 Samuel 13:20-29). Instead, Absalom contended that it was David's fault. "Why didn't my father punish Amnon? If he would have done what he was supposed to do, I wouldn't have had to bring vengeance upon Amnon for what he did to my sister!" Once Amnon was dead, Absalom went into a self-imposed exile for three years because he was afraid of what would happen to him for the murder of his brother (2 Samuel 13:37-38).

Lessons from David:

David allowed Absalom to come back to the nation of Israel, but for two whole years he didn't see him (2 Samuel 14:21-24, 28). Finally, Absalom imposed upon Joab to get him an audience with the king. Although David came in and hugged and kissed Absalom, it doesn't mention that they reconciled. David didn't say, "Well, everything's okay now."

After David refused to whitewash what had happened, Absalom began his treason and eventually caused a civil war. He tried to kill his own father and then committed adultery with his father's concubines openly in broad daylight (2 Samuel 15-18).

Absalom was full of hatred and blamed his father for all of his woes, saying, "It's because David didn't punish Amnon that I've done these things. It's because David didn't accept me back. It's because David allowed this thing to go on that we're where we are." Absalom felt justified in doing what he was doing. He felt like he was getting vengeance on his father for ruining his life.

Defying Logic

This is an important difference between David, Saul, and Absalom. David never transposed his problems onto other people. He accepted responsibility for his actions. Saul and Absalom didn't.

One of the most important issues facing our society today is that people will not accept responsibility for their actions. Nobody will say, "It's my fault." We're probably all heard the story about the woman who purchased boiling hot coffee from the McDonald's drive thru, put it between her legs, and drove off. Then when the coffee splashed out and burned her, instead of saying, "That was stupid. I burned myself. How could I have done this?"—she sued McDonald's because the coffee was "too hot." That's crazy enough, but then the jury blamed McDonald's and made them pay for damages that were actually a result of this woman's own stupid actions.

Today if someone gets killed with a gun, it's not the fault of the person who pulled the trigger. The company that manufactured the gun is now blamed for this death. Guns don't kill people any more than forks make people fat! We're saying cigarette companies are responsible for people smoking cigarettes. We're saying fast food chains are responsible for our obesity claiming, "They should have put a warning label on their food telling me I shouldn't eat here every single day, three meals a day." That's just stupid! It defies logic! You can't blame somebody else for the stupid things you do. You have a responsibility over your own life.

No longer is a person responsible for being an alcoholic or a drug addict, it's because they have a genetic predisposition. People contend that genes control whether someone will become an addicted gambler or not. They say, "Gambling is an addiction. I can't control it. I just happen to be inferior to other people." They say the same thing about emotional issues like depression. "It's not me. It's not my choices. It's just a chemical imbalance. Give me a pill and put me into a stupor to control my emotions."

I know there are people who get very upset with me because I say that it's not genetics or chemical imbalances that cause depression, alcoholism, gambling, or drug addiction. They say,

Lessons from David:

"Who are you? All of these educated 'experts' have done all of these studies." I don't care how many degrees someone has after their name or how they became deified in the secular world. If what they say is contrary to the Word, they're wrong!

Always Rejoice!

Let God be true, but every man a liar.

Romans 3:4

God's Word is a greater authority in my life than what anybody else has to say. In fact, the Word teaches us that the Lord will hold us accountable for our emotions. My book entitled, *Harnessing Your Emotions,* goes into much more detail on this topic. God made us accountable for our emotions and actually punished people for not rejoicing.

Because thou servedst not the LORD thy God with joyfulness, and with gladness of heart, for the abundance of all things; therefore shalt thou serve thine enemies which the LORD shall send against thee.

Deuteronomy 28:47–48

As born-again believers, the Lord doesn't send enemies against us. However, we can open up a door for the devil by grumbling and complaining. That's why we're commanded to:

Rejoice in the Lord always: and again I say, Rejoice.

Philippians 4:4

Emphasizing this word "always," Psalm 34:1 says:

I will bless the Lord at all times: his praise shall continually be in my mouth.

(emphasis mine)

Not Troubled by Trouble

On the night before His crucifixion, Jesus told His disciples that they would have trouble but they should not be troubled by it.

In the world ye shall have tribulation: but be of good cheer; I have overcome the world.

John 16:33; emphasis mine

The Lord acknowledged tribulation. He didn't just say, "Be of good cheer when everything goes good. I'm going to remove all of your problems so that you'll never have a reason to be discouraged ever again." No, He was saying, "There will be tribulation. But in the midst of that negative circumstance, be of good cheer!"

If you or someone you know is facing a crisis situation, I recommend my teaching entitled, *The Christian Survival Kit.* This is an in-depth study of John 14, 15, and 16, which contain Jesus' last words to His disciples before His arrest and crucifixion. These messages have helped many people overcome.

This mindset of not accepting responsibility has spread like a cancer throughout our society. It has even infected Christians. We say, "It's because they said this about me; I was born into an underprivileged home; it's because of the color of my skin; I don't have an education; or the devil made me do it." And if you can't find something else to blame your actions on, just blame it on your dysfunctional family. It's totally subjective. However, God would be unjust to command us to do something that we are incapable of doing, either because of circumstances or because of genetics.

You can justify murder, rape, adultery—anything—because of the way you were potty trained, because you didn't get a birthday cake when you were three, or any of a myriad of other things. That's absurd! It's unbelievable that people fall for that, yet it's being said so often in our society that even Christians are being influenced by it. That's absolutely wrong!

If you want to be a person after God's own heart, you're going to have to unplug from the way this world thinks, quit excusing your actions, and accept responsibility. David humbled himself and said, "God, it's me! I'm the one who sinned." This is one of the heart attitudes that stand out in stark contrast to both Saul and Absalom. David accepted responsibility for his own actions.

Chapter 13

A Snare

Accepting responsibility is one of the greatest signs of true repentance. David humbled himself, accepted responsibility, and refused to blame anybody else. Saul eventually admitted, "I've sinned," because he was forced to (1 Samuel 15:24). However, he was still pointing the finger saying, "But you don't understand. The people did this. It's their fault!" Saul hadn't truly repented.

The prodigal son truly repented. Notice what he purposed in his heart to tell his father:

I will arise and go to my father, and will say unto him, Father, I have sinned against heaven, and before thee. And am no more worthy to be called thy son: make me as one of thy hired servants.

Luke 15:18-19

He was saying, "Father, I was wrong and I don't have any justification. I don't have any claim on your goodness. I have voided everything, but I'm asking for mercy." He didn't come to his father and say, "I think I've made a mistake, but it's your fault too. You shouldn't have given me all that money. You shouldn't have allowed this to happen. You're the one who drove me away. You're the one who gave me my inheritance early!" He didn't point the finger at his father and say, "You don't understand what happened when I was in this foreign land. People took advantage of me. I had to eat pig's food just to survive!" No, the prodigal son truly repented. He didn't try to blame things on anyone else. He took responsibility for his own actions.

Failure to accept responsibility and pointing the finger while saying, "It's someone else's fault!" is a sure sign that a heart hasn't changed and there isn't genuine repentance. I've seen many people in the Christian community who got in trouble and had their sins exposed, whether moral, ethical, or civil. Perhaps they were going to lose something like their spouse or family or maybe they had to go to court or jail because of what they did. I've seen people who were humiliated, who cried, who said they were sorry and they repented, but there was this thread running through everything they said: "Yes, I'm wrong. I can't believe I did this. But you just don't understand. I was raised to be this way. My family was always like this. This person drove me to do this. With the way my spouse treated me, I just couldn't help it." As long as there remain little threads of blame, genuine heartfelt repentance hasn't occurred yet. They are only sorry they got caught. In order to be a person after God's own heart, you're going to have to move beyond that.

A Snare

What David Wanted

Unlike Saul and Absalom, David didn't care about anyone else's opinion. He was a God pleaser, not a man pleaser. The Lord was foremost in his life. Let that sink in for a moment. God can't be seen. As far as the physical realm is concerned, He's intangible. But when David humbled himself before God and repented of his sin with Bathsheba, he said:

I have sinned against the LORD.

2 Samuel 12:13

Against thee, thee only, have I sinned, and done this evil in thy sight.

Psalm 51:4

David confessed, "Against You and You only, Lord, have I sinned!" God's opinion of him was the only thing he was concerned about. There is no indication in the Scripture that David ever just publicly told everybody everything that had happened, but there is also zero indication that he hid it. He exposed himself and brought his sin out in the open. David didn't do this in an imprudent way. He didn't just go around every day asking everyone, "Have you heard yet what I've done?" But he didn't try to conceal it or cover it up, either. David wanted relationship with God more than man's approval.

"It's Over!"

Contrast this with Saul. In the second half of 1 Samuel 15:23, Samuel continued his reproof of Saul saying:

Lessons from David:

Because thou hast rejected the word of the LORD, he hath also rejected thee from being king.

Then Saul responded:

I have sinned: for I have transgressed the commandment of the LORD, and thy words: because I feared the people, and obeyed their voice.

1 Samuel 15:24

Saul was forced to admit, "Alright, I'm wrong. But it was the people who made me do it!" He was still pointing the finger. There wasn't genuine repentance. He still refused to take responsibility for his own actions.

Now therefore, I pray thee, pardon my sin, and turn again with me, that I may worship the LORD. And Samuel said unto Saul, I will not return with thee: for thou hast rejected the word of the LORD, and the LORD hath rejected thee from being king over Israel.

1 Samuel 15:25-26

In our day and age, people are elected president and as long as they have their popularity—or force—they can maintain their position. But this was a theocracy. Saul had been chosen by God to rule, but he only had this power as long as the Lord gave it to him. Here was the messenger of God saying, "It's over! You've lost everything. Not only are you going to cease to be king, but your children will never inherit the kingdom. Your dynasty is over. God is going to raise up another king." Now that's a severe judgment!

A Snare

Man Pleaser

And as Samuel turned about to go away, he [Saul] laid hold upon the skirt of his [Samuel's] mantle, and it rent. And Samuel said unto him, The LORD hath rent the kingdom of Israel from thee this day, and hath given it to a neighbour of thine, that is better than thou.

1 Samuel 15:27–28; brackets mine

Right after he received the judgment that the kingdom was taken away from him, Saul grabbed Samuel's robe and it tore. Samuel used that as a word picture to illustrate what God had just done in the spirit as he told Saul, "God just tore the kingdom right out of your hand!" Look how Saul reacted to this terrible judgment pronounced upon him:

Then he said, I have sinned: yet honour me now, I pray thee, before the elders of my people, and before Israel, and turn again with me, that I may worship the Lord thy God.

1 Samuel 15:30

Do you see what Saul was doing? He said, "Alright, I've lost the kingdom. God has rejected me. He's punishing me, but that's not really what's important in my life. Please honor me so I'll still look good in the sight of the people!"

Saul's problem was that he was a man pleaser. The evidence is right here. He had lost everything but instead of repenting and saying, "Lord, forgive me! How could I do this? I love You more than anything else. I must have Your acceptance," he was willing to let all that go. The main issue for Saul wasn't the Lord's favor, but rather honor in the sight of the people.

Are You a God Pleaser?

God's Word is very clear about this.

The fear of man bringeth a snare: but whoso putteth his trust in the LORD shall be safe.

Proverbs 29:25

Being a man pleaser brings a snare. A snare is a trap that was used to catch animals and birds. Satan goes about "seeking whom he may devour" (1 Peter 5:8). When we become a man pleaser, we open the door for the enemy to come in and devour us. This happens when we seek to receive our approval and validation from people more than God. We need to seek first God's kingdom and His righteousness (Matthew 6:33). We need to seek the Lord's acceptance and approval more than man's acceptance and approval. Make God first place in your life. Be more concerned about pleasing Him than your own reputation. That's how you can avoid this trap of the devil.

In a sense, we've all become the politicians that we abhor. Many politicians—not all, but many—constantly keep their finger in the air to check which way the public opinion polls are blowing. And whatever it is that the people want to hear, that's what they have to say. They're like chameleons, void of any convictions of their own. They change and do whatever will buy them enough votes to get them re-elected. They're out to please people one hundred percent of the time! They have no integrity. You can't tell what they're going to do in a particular situation because it just depends on what the polls show at that particular time. That's terrible!

You're probably thinking that I'm right in saying this is wrong; that we ought to be people of convictions. But may I ask you a personal question? Is that the way you are? It's easy for us to judge politicians, but what about you? If you were applying for a job or a promotion at work and you had to be really candid about something in your background that might affect whether you receive the job or promotion, would you be honest and open about it? If you were applying for a loan, would you tell the bankers the things they want to know, even if they could be used against you? Are you a God pleaser or a man pleaser?

If I was being considered for a job and had something in my past like a police record, I wouldn't conceal it. I would be open and honest and tell people up front. I am not a man pleaser. My security is in God. Because of this, I'm secure. I'm safe. The Lord is my Provider, and He will provide me with a job (Psalm 90:16-17).

Completely Transparent

This is a major difference between David and many Christians today. David humbled himself and accepted responsibility for what he did. He didn't try to cover it up or blame someone else. David was so God conscious that it didn't matter to him if the entire nation knew of his sin. What mattered to him was getting his relationship with God back to where it should be.

Lessons from David:

To be a person after God's own heart, you need to quit covering up, hiding, and concealing sin and failure in your life. Of course you need to use wisdom. Don't just go out there and announce your sin like it's something you're proud of. But if you're applying for something and they expect you to put down any past problems you've had, be honest. Trust God and tell them the truth.

The Bible doesn't say, "You shall not lie." It says, "You shall not bear false witness" (Exodus 20:16). If you're filling out an application and it asks for a past history and you fail to put something there that should be, you just given false witness. You may say, "But I didn't lie!" Well, yes, you did. You gave a false representation of yourself. You need to be candid. Don't carry a sign down the street that says, "I've committed adultery" or "I went to prison," but if something needs to be said, be honest and courageous enough to expose it to light.

Sometimes you need to tell someone about your past sins in order to help them. Perhaps somebody you are dealing with has a similar problem to what you've had. You desire to keep these dark things concealed in your life and don't want them to be known. But if you shared them, you could minister hope and encouragement to someone. You could testify of how the Lord forgave you, how He healed your heart, or how He restored your marriage. If you won't share something just because you don't want anyone else to know about it, then you're still a man pleaser. You're still ensnared by the fear of man.

Jesus spoke the truth. He didn't enjoy upsetting people. He didn't rebuke because He loved controversy, strife, and criticism. Some of today's talk shows just love controversy because it sells.

It draws people in. It improves their ratings. The Lord wasn't like that. Jesus was absolutely free to tell the truth to people who had the authority to hurt him (Luke 22:66-23:3). He was fearless. There were no snares in His life because He didn't care about man's opinion. Jesus was out to only please His Father. That's how we need to be too. We need to be completely transparent.

Be Who God Wants You to Be!

Are you willing to do anything the Lord wants? Will you maintain your integrity in the face of negative peer pressure from your fellow employees, or if it means possibly being passed over for a promotion at work? Do you have that kind of attitude?

I remember hearing a fifteen-year-old girl give a testimony at the local church I attend. For the past two years of her Christian life, she had been living a life of compromise. She hated who she had become and what she was doing. However, she wanted to be accepted by certain peers.

She went on a mission trip to Costa Rica and while there, she visited a girls' home. She met young ladies who had been beaten and raped, were impoverished, and had all kinds of disadvantages. This caused her to realize how blessed she really was. The Lord had given her a good home, loving parents, and a wonderful church. She began to feel ashamed of the fact that she wanted the approval of these other teenagers more than God. All of a sudden, it just clicked inside of her and she declared, "I'm going to start being true to myself. I'm going to be who I want to be and more importantly, who

God wants me to be!" In a sense, she was saying, "I'm going to start pleasing God more than people." This was a tremendous testimony of something that most adult believers have never grasped. This young girl was choosing to be a God pleaser instead of a man pleaser.

David lived to please God, but Saul and Absalom lived to please man. If you want to become a person after God's own heart, you have to get to the place where you love God and value His acceptance and approval more than man's. When David was reproved for his sin, what broke his heart was how he had broken his relationship with God. He didn't care what anyone else thought. He wanted that relationship with God back more than anything. It didn't matter about his kingdom. Let somebody else take it; he didn't care. David just wanted God.

Saul didn't value his relationship with God that way. When the Lord forsook him, quit responding to him, and wouldn't answer him, Saul just went and consulted a witch (1 Samuel 28:3-19). He didn't care how he got his answer. His relationship with God just wasn't that important. Saul wanted results. This is exactly the reason why many people aren't men or women after God's own heart today.

Chapter 14

A Purpose Bigger than Yourself

D avid was a man after God's own heart. This wasn't always obvious from his actions, but it was definitely evidenced by the attitude of his heart. David accepted responsibility and was accountable for his actions. He always sought God's acceptance and approval, not man's. David had a cause that was bigger than himself.

In other words, David wasn't the center of his universe. He wasn't the focus of his own life. David knew he was where he was to serve God's purposes, not his own. He didn't just use God to get his way, but longed for the Lord to use him to accomplish His purposes. This important trait helped make David a man after God's own heart.

If you live a self-centered life, you will never be a person after God's own heart. Take, for instance, the business realm. If you're running neck and neck with someone for a promotion at work, are you thinking of what's best for the company or is your attitude, *Who cares about the company—what's best for me? I need this promotion. I need this money. What about me? What about my ego?* This self-serving, self-centered kind of attitude is completely inconsistent with God's heart. If you are all wrapped up in yourself, you make a very small package!

I have a book entitled, *Self-Centeredness: The Source of All Grief.* This book goes into much more detail about this. I encourage you to get it!

The Ark Stays

David didn't have a selfish attitude. Serving God benefited and promoted David in life. It brought him from being a shepherd boy to being king. But this was just a fringe benefit. These things came as by-products of his relationship with God. David's heart was to serve the Lord.

Even when Absalom revolted against him, David's heart was to serve the Lord. Absalom invested years into winning over the hearts of the people. He was a handsome, gifted individual, and the people loved him. He literally stole the people's hearts away from his father, David (2 Samuel 15:6). Absalom invited certain nobles to join with him and proclaimed himself king. When David got wind of this, he had to flee for his life from Jerusalem, or he would have been trapped there and killed by Absalom (2 Samuel 15:13-14). While leaving with those still loyal to him...

The king said unto Zadok [the priest], Carry back the ark of God into the city: if I shall find favour in the eyes of the LORD, he will bring me again, and show me both it, and his habitation: but if he thus say, I have no delight in thee; behold, here am I, let him do to me as seemeth good unto him.

2 Samuel 15:25-26

What a tremendous passage of scripture! What a revelation into David's heart. David was fleeing for his life, fleeing from the shame brought on by his own son's rebellion against him. Yet when he had opportunity to take the Ark, which would have given him a great advantage, with him, David said, "No. Take the Ark back to its place in the tabernacle. If God is pleased to return me as king over Israel, then I'll come back to it. But if the Lord is through with me, then let Him do what He wants." In other words David was saying, "If God wants me to be king, I'll come back to Jerusalem and the Ark. But if not, let the Ark stay here and serve God's people."

David had a purpose that was bigger than himself. Although he was king, he did not view the position as an opportunity to boost his ego or benefit him. David was king to serve the Lord and the nation of Israel. This was God's call on his life. When David stepped up to the plate when his nation was impoverished and oppressed by the Philistines, he didn't fight Goliath for himself, but to serve God by overcoming the armies of the Philistines to bring deliverance to the Israelites. David was king for the same reason—to serve God and His people. That was his purpose. David wasn't just consumed with self. Self was not the god of his life!

Lessons from David:

Focus on the Message!

In order to truly understand what it means to reject self as the god of your life, the Holy Spirit must reveal it to you. This trait will make you a person after God's own heart. You must die to yourself and come alive to something that's bigger than you. There are so many ways we're all tempted to exalt ourselves in everyday situations. If you can overcome in the small things, you'll be able to handle the big temptations when they come.

The year 2003 marked the twenty-fifth anniversary of the incorporation of Andrew Wommack Ministries. It was also the thirty-fifth anniversary of God supernaturally touching my life. We produced an anniversary magazine detailing some of the things the Lord had done. We also stated our vision for the future in this magazine.

As we were preparing this magazine, members of our production department came to me with a list of questions they wanted Jamie and me to answer. Some of the questions were: "What is your favorite color? What are your hobbies? What do you like to do on your days off?" I understand that these are questions that people would want to ask a leader in a newspaper type of article, but I had to tell them, "Look, I understand what you're doing, but you're missing something here. This ministry isn't about me. It's not about what my favorite color is or what I like to do in my free time. This is about the message God has given me to share with the entire world!"

All of our ministry expansion, including this new building and the multiplying of Bible colleges all around the world, isn't about me.

It's not about me looking at something and saying, "Look what I've built." No! All of these things are just tools to get the job done. The important thing is getting the Word out about God's unconditional love and the balance of grace and faith. The reason I get excited when I see the new building, our schools multiplying and growing, and new radio and television stations added is because the message the Lord has put in my heart to share is changing people's lives. It's exciting to accomplish what God has called us to do!

I have a purpose that's bigger than me. It's not about having a large facility, being recognized by millions of people, or anything like that. It's about the message! That's why I redirected my staff and said, "Ask me questions about the ministry, how it started, some of the hardships we've been through, and lessons we've learned that could help someone else overcome their hardships, but keep this publication focused on the message." We must always stay focused on the message—not the messenger!

A Man of Purpose

I use a lot of personal examples when I minister. In fact, I just used one in the last few paragraphs. But my purpose in doing this isn't to bring attention to myself, but rather to illustrate my points. I've found that personal examples are one of the best ways people can relate to, understand, and apply the message I'm trying to communicate.

Ronald Reagan was one of the best presidents we've ever had. He is credited with ending the Cold War, among many other things. Although I don't necessarily agree with everything he did, he was a great president. As he was leaving public office, he received a tremendous amount of recognition. As people started thinking about his legacy, one of the questions often directed toward President Reagan concerned what made him such a great man. Almost every time, without fail, he responded by saying, "There's nothing great about me. I'm an ordinary person—but I had an extraordinary message! I'm not a great man. I'm a man who had great ideas and great purpose!"

Ronald Reagan wasn't out to build his legacy. He had a philosophy and a goal of less government and more personal responsibility. He had a vision of overcoming the Soviet Union and the Cold War problems through strength and refusal to back down. It wasn't just détente or business as usual. Reagan's purpose—which was bigger than himself—drove him and caused him to succeed.

In the same manner, my God-given purpose motivates and spurs me on. The Lord touched me and changed my life. He burned a revelation in my heart, and I'm doing everything I can to get this message out. These truths I'm sharing about David have become real to me and have transformed my life. I believe the Lord wants them to become real to you and impact your life and the lives of millions of others too. That's what drives me!

If I were in ministry just for my own personal benefit, I would have quit a long time ago. It's true, we are prospering and enjoying a certain measure of success right now. However, I've been in ministry now for over forty-five years. We've lived through decades of hardships and trials. If this was about me, I would have given up and changed careers decades ago. There are other ways I could have provided for my family. I could have done something else and made a mark. But this isn't about me. It's about serving the Lord and accomplishing His goals. I have a God-given purpose that is bigger than myself!

"I Choose to Serve God"

This is one of the reasons why David was a man after God's own heart. When David's life, kingdom and legacy were literally on the line, what mattered to David was serving God. He didn't care about all those other things. He said, "If it pleases God and that's what's best for the nation, then I'll come back. But if the Lord is through with me and it's better for the nation that I be gone and Absalom rule, then that's fine with me!"

I can truthfully testify to you today that if God were to tell me that I was doing more damage than good, and it was better for the body of Christ that I do something else besides minister, I would. I'm not saying that I would completely like it. I wouldn't necessarily enjoy it any more than David enjoyed facing death and having his own son try to kill him. I'm not saying it would be pleasant. But I can honestly say that if I felt that it was to the kingdom of God's advantage that I no longer minister, then I would get out of the ministry. If it would please God and glorify Him to use someone else and to have me promote them and help them succeed ahead of me, I would do it with all my heart. Not many people can say that!

What about you? Have you been accepting responsibility for

your actions or do you still shift the blame? Are you claiming that something or someone else is to blame for your difficulties - your dysfunctional family, hormones, genetics, chemical imbalance, or the like? Examine your heart.

If you've been guilty of any of these things, you can repent and start changing your heart. You can begin by dying to yourself and saying, "Lord, please help me get to the place where serving, exalting, and pleasing You is more important to me than doing my own thing." If you honestly do this, the process of change will begin.

You can change your heart, but you can't do it by yourself. God has to change your heart. It requires His power, but it's your choice whether that power functions or not. You must stop exalting yourself and living by your own self-will. Quit acting like Saul and saying, "It's their fault. They made me do it!" or "I don't care if I lose everything from God, just make me look good in the eyes of people." Stop acting like Absalom and saying, "It's all my father's, mother's, sister's, brother's—somebody else's fault. It's not mine!" You aren't accepting the fact that you are the one who started this whole process. You're simply shifting blame so you feel justified.

This is nothing more than vengeance on your part. That's not operating like a person after God's own heart. You need to change that! The good news is you can change. It starts with a decision, but it doesn't end there. You have to walk it out.

Cultivate a Sensitive Heart

The contrasts between these three kings really brings out and magnifies the traits that made David a man after God's own heart and it reveals how you and I can become people after God's own heart today. But the choice is up to you. You choose what your heart is going to be like.

Whatever your heart is like right now is the result of the choices you have made in the past. You might not have intentionally and with understanding said, "I want to be a hard-hearted person," but you have made choices that have hardened your heart toward God. You can start making choices today that will soften and sensitize your heart toward God. My book entitled, *Hardness of Heart*, goes right along with this. It instructs you on how to cultivate and keep a a heart that is sensitive toward the Lord.

Lessons from David:

Chapter 15

Follow God's Order

The Ark of the Covenant was made in Moses' day, approximately 400 years before David's story. By the time David was crowned king, it had been sitting for years in Abinadab's house, in Kirjathjearim (1 Samuel 7:1), or what is called Gibeah (2 Samuel 6:3).

After David was crowned king, he intended to bring the Ark of the Covenant to Jerusalem, the city he had chosen as his royal city and residence. The Ark symbolized God's presence, and it didn't seem good to him not to have it in Jerusalem (1 Chronicles 13:2-3). So David had the Ark placed on a cart that was pulled by oxen, and they started for Jerusalem. It was a great company of people, and they were rejoicing and praising God with instruments. But while they were on the way, something terrible happened—

And when they came to Nachon's threshingfloor, Uzzah put forth his hand to the ark of God, and took hold of it; for the oxen shook it. And the anger of the LORD was kindled against Uzzah; and God smote him there for his error; and there he died by the ark of God.

2 Samuel 6:6-7

Lessons from David:

This judgment upon Uzzah seems harsh and the Scripture says, "David was displeased, because the Lᴏʀᴅ had made a breach upon Uzzah" (2 Samuel 6:8). You might be able to identify with David here. I know many people who feel like God failed them and they are mad at Him or at least displeased with Him as David was, but God is never wrong.

There was a reason for what happened. David didn't know what that reason was at the time, but he later realized he had missed it instead of God. We should learn a lesson from David here. From our point of view, it sometimes looks like God's promises aren't true, but that's never the case. If some of His promises didn't come to pass, you can count on the fact that there was something the Lord told us to do that we failed to do. Never forget that!

David didn't realize it, but there was a prescribed order as to how the Ark was supposed to be approached and handled (Numbers 4:15). The Ark had to be kept behind a veil in a place called the "holy of holies," which was in the tabernacle. On either side of the mercy seat of the Ark were two gold cherubims—warrior angels. They were there as a symbol to let people know that angels kept people from the presence of God. This was intended to depict the separation between a "holy God" and "unholy man."

Only the high priest could go in to where the Ark was, and he could only do that once a year to make atonement for the people's sins and for his own sins (Leviticus 16:34). If he didn't do everything just right in there, God would smite him. A first-century historian named Josephus recorded that they actually had a rope tied around the high priest's ankle with the end of it trailing out beyond the veil.

146

That way if the priest was struck dead while in the holy of holies, they could drag him out. They certainly couldn't go in after him to get him or they would be struck dead too!

When Jesus made atonement for our sins, this veil that seperated man from the Ark was rent in two (Matthew 27:51). Now we have direct access to God! But in the Old Testament, this separation between a holy God and unholy man had to be enforced. People couldn't just approach God. None of us are worthy. "All have sinned, and come short of the glory of God" (Romans 3:23).

There are a lot of people today who don't understand and appreciate these things and they talk about God in a way that doesn't reverence Him. They think God is love (1 John 4:8), therefore He will just accept them. But God is a holy God too! The only reason we have access to Him today is because a price was paid. The Scripture says that "the wages of sin is death" (Romans 6:23). A price had to be paid and before that price was paid, man could not just come into the presence of God.

There Is a Prescribed Order

God had specific instructions about how to handle the Ark of the Covenant. It was to be carried between two poles by the Levites so that it would be supported properly and couldn't fall (Exodus 25:12-15 and Numbers 4). This also kept it out of reach so no one could bump into it and bring judgment on themselves. But David was bringing the Ark to Jerusalem on a cart that could easily bounce and tip over, and sure enough, that's exactly what happened. The oxen stumbled and the Ark was about to fall over. Then Uzzah, trying to brace it, reached out and touched it—totally violating God's prescribed order. So God struck him dead!

Sin's price had not yet been paid, so no one could touch the presence of God and get away with it. David got very upset when Uzzah was struck dead. His intentions were good. The Lord could have adjusted His rules, but that's not how it works.

Sometimes we are tempted to think that the Lord is too bound to His word. Our intentions are good, so we think He should just perform our every wish even though we are full of doubt or fear or bitterness or whatever. But we have to conform our actions to God's standards, not the other way around. The next verse says:

And David was afraid of the LORD that day, and said, How shall the ark of the LORD come to me?

2 Samuel 6:9

David humbled himself before the Lord. That's one of the qualities that made him a man after God's own heart (1 Samuel 13:14). Instead of being mad, David feared the Lord. David quickly realized there's only one God—and he wasn't Him! That's a very wise thing to do when it looks like God's not coming through for us. We should humble ourselves and proclaim God's faithfulness, even when it doesn't look like He's been faithful to us.

David had the Ark moved to Obed-Edom's house. After three months, he was told that Obed-Edom was being blessed because of the Ark. So once again David wanted to bring the Ark to Jerusalem. He said,

Follow God's Order

None ought to carry the ark of God but the Levites: for them hath the LORD chosen to carry the ark of God, and to minister unto him for ever.

1 Chronicles 15:2

This indicates that David had finally gone back and asked God, "What happened with Uzzah? Why didn't this work?" He went back to God's Word and found the proper way to carry the Ark. David revealed to the Levites what God told him:

Ye are the chief of the fathers of the Levites: sanctify yourselves, both ye and your brethren, that ye may bring up the ark of the LORD God of Israel unto the place that I have prepared for it. For because ye did it not at the first, the LORD our God made a breach upon us, for that we sought him not after the due order.

1 Chronicles 15:12-13

Uzzah died because David didn't follow God's prescribed order. He hadn't sought the Lord the first time about how to handle the Ark. There are a lot of applications I can make from this, but one of them is that many people, even so-called Christians, say, "It doesn't matter how you seek the Lord. You can be a Buddhist, a Hindu, a Muslim, or whatever. There's only one God, but there are many paths that lead to Him. Just as long as you believe in some divine being and as long as you do your best, that's good enough." Boy, if you are paying attention to this example from David's life, you can see that there is a proper order to seeking the Lord. David desired a good end but because he didn't do it the proper way, a man died needlessly.

Lessons from David:

I have talked to many people who had this same attitude that it doesn't matter the way you get there, just as long as you believe there's a God. Others believe that God is a good God so He's going to accept them regardless of which way they choose. That's not right. There is a right way and a wrong way to relate to God.

Neither is there salvation in any other: for there is no other name under heaven given among men, whereby we must be saved.

Acts 4:12

I [Jesus] am the way, the truth, and the life: no man cometh unto the Father, but by me.

John 14:6; brackets mine

Just Ask Uzzah

Most people do not let the Bible get in the way of what they believe. But if you're going to really connect with the Lord, the Bible is the instruction manual. It is God telling you how to relate to Him, and you have to do it according to the pattern He gives. That's really simple, but I guarantee you there are a lot of people today who have accepted the mindset that they can relate to God any way they want.

That's what David started off thinking. He wanted to do something good but he thought that it didn't really matter whether he followed the instructions of the Word of God. A cart can travel faster than a man. It was going to be a long trip, and it'd be much easier for the oxen to carry the Ark than for people to carry it. But quick and easy isn't always the best way. The Bible prescribes the way to do things. Just ask Uzzah! You need to accept the Word of God and recognize that there's a reason He gives the instructions He gives.

David finally saw that and transported the Ark the way God told him, so the Scripture goes on to say:

> *So David went and brought up the ark of God from the house of Obededom into the city of David with gladness. And it was so, that when they that bare the ark of the LORD had gone six paces, he sacrificed oxen and fatlings. And David danced before the LORD with all his might; and David was girded with a linen ephod. So David and all the house of Israel brought up the ark of the LORD with shouting, and with the sound of the trumpet.*
>
> *2 Samuel 6:12-15*

David went back to praising God! He didn't stop worshiping because of this incident with Uzzah. Things just work out when you do it God's way! This is a major lesson to learn from the life of David. Do it God's way—the first time—and you'll avoid unnecessary problems.

"Frankly, I Don't Give a Rip!"

And as the ark of the LORD came into the city of David, Michal Saul's daughter looked through a window, and saw

Lessons from David:

king David leaping and dancing before the LORD; and she despised him in her heart.

2 Samuel 6:16

Michal was David's wife. She had been given to him by Saul, the previous king who was her father. Saul had given Michal to David to be a snare to him (1 Samuel 18:21), implying that this woman probably had some really bad attitudes. Saul saw giving Michal to David as a punishment. But the Scripture says Michal loved David (1 Samuel 18:20), and she saved his life from her father (1 Samuel 19:11-18). Then Saul took her and gave her to be the wife of Phalti (1 Samuel 25:44). Women during those days were treated as property and had no choice in matters like this.

When David became king, probably thirteen or fourteen years later, he took Michal from her husband (2 Samuel 3:14-15). The Scriptures don't give us all the details, but it's obvious she was hurt by this. Here was a king's daughter—a princess—who had been married to a man she loved and then ripped from him and given to another man. By the time David took her back, she had probably adjusted and even learned to love Phalti. In other words, she was over David. She probably thought to herself, "Why did you take me from my husband after it's been so long? Where were you when I was given to Phalti? Where have you been?" She might have even been jealous that David had since married and she had to share him with his other wives. She was used to having a husband only to herself.

This instance in 2 Samuel 6 makes it obvious that Michal was bitter over the abuse that had happened in her life. When she saw David dancing and twirling around, she directed this bitterness at him. The Scripture says "she despised him in her heart." She didn't wait for David to come to her. She was hot. She went out to meet him and began criticizing him, saying,

How glorious was the king of Israel to day, who uncovered himself to day in the eyes of the handmaids of his servants, as one of the vain fellows shamelessly uncovereth himself!

2 Samuel 6:20

This was totally sarcastic of her. She thought David was ruining the kingship. Her father had certainly never acted like David was acting. But the truth is that Saul would never have danced before the Lord like this because he was a man pleaser, not a God pleaser. David was a completely different king than Saul was. What he was doing was for the Lord! But Michal didn't recognize that.

When Michal said David shamelessly uncovered himself, she meant he uncovered himself in an improper way. It's possible that he took off an outer garment but was totally clothed while he was dancing. In his exuberance, he might have exposed something he wasn't supposed to reveal, but she was unjustly criticizing him. And here is his response:

It was before the LORD, which chose me before thy father, and before all his house, to appoint me ruler over the people of the LORD, over Israel: therefore will I play before the LORD. And I will yet be more vile than thus, and will be base in mine own

Lessons from David:

sight: and of the maidservants which thou hast spoken of, of them shall I be had in honour.

2 Samuel 6:21-22

Regardless of the injustices done to her, Michal didn't get a pass for criticizing David. He was the one who was worshiping God! She totally missed praising God and was blinded by her bitterness. This is one of the things that made David a man after God's own heart: He loved God and wasn't ashamed to show his commitment and affection to Him publicly. He basically said, "I was worshiping God, and frankly, I don't give a rip what people think! I was doing this for the Lord, and I'll become even more undignified than this!" Contrary to what Michal thought, he had learned to do things the prescribed way. He wasn't going to stop worshiping God for anything! He referred to how God had blessed him, and he was not ashamed to show his love, his commitment, and his worship to God in front of people. This has direct implications to our lives also.

If you want to be a man or a woman after God's own heart, you need to learn that your love and commitment to God ought to trump any other relationship. You shouldn't be a man pleaser, no matter what. David was thankful that God had allowed him to take the Ark—literally, His presence—into Jerusalem. Everybody should have been shouting about this!

Stand Up for the Lord

In John 5:44, Jesus said,

How can ye believe, which receive honour one of another, and seek not the honour that cometh from God only?

People act like they have never read this. Most don't realize that being a man pleaser stops them from believing God. They are intimidated by what other people think. They are afraid to stand up for what His Word says. And you know what? They are exactly opposite of how David was here. I'm not saying you should attack people who are ungodly. Of course you should love them, but you should not be ashamed to stand up for the Lord and His standards.

David didn't care that he was thought of as a fool for showing that kind of affection and commitment to God. He turned the tables on this criticism. This is one of the lessons you can learn from David. You shouldn't feel strange or intimidated by people who don't love God, whose standards are totally wrong. They are the ones who ought to feel strange. You're not the weird one—they are! You're the one who loves God and believes that He's alive and that miracles happen. That's normal! You shouldn't be the one who feels awkward and out of place.

Look at what happened to David and Michal after this:

Therefore Michal the daughter of Saul had no child unto the day of her death.

2 Samuel 6:23

In other words, that was the end of her relationship with David.

Lessons from David:

She let this bitterness ruin her relationship with the man after God's own heart. She had some bad things happen to her, but she vented this bitterness and it cost her dearly for the rest of her life.

Here's another lesson that you can learn from this situation. You may have had bad things happen to you, but you have a choice as to whether you'll become bitter or better. If you allow this bitterness to fester, the Scripture says that a root of bitterness will spring up and defile the whole body and many people will be defiled because of it (Hebrews 12:15). You need to run to the Lord and let Him take care of any bitterness you might have. You don't need to spew it out because it'll keep you from being fruitful the rest of your life. There are a lot of things to learn here, but you don't have to learn them from your own hard knocks. The Bible is full of examples like this one to show you how to do things and be who He's called you to be.

Chapter 16

The Danger of Prosperity

Although David had many great and godly accomplishments, he also experienced a great downfall. The man after God's own heart sinned and transgressed against the Lord.

The Bible is very candid, even when dealing with major characters like David. Instead of glossing over his failures, it's very plain. The Lord's purpose for this was to benefit you and me today. We can learn many lessons, even from the negative aspects of David's life.

Have you ever been through a major moral failure? If so, there are some things in David's life that can help you recover, especially when you see how God dealt with him and was able to continue using him. If not, then you can receive instruction through David's life regarding how much his sin cost him and damaged those around him. It will definitely inspire you not to go that route. So whether you've been through a major moral failure in your life or not, there are lessons God wants you to learn from David.

When David sinned with Bathsheba, he didn't just make a mistake. It wasn't that he just momentarily gave in to his humanity and failed in one small area. David literally turned from God

Lessons from David:

and went the other way. He rebelled. David didn't have a major departure from God "accidentally." There were reasons why this happened.

Sin Must Be Conceived

But every man is tempted, when he is drawn away of his own lust, and enticed. Then when lust hath conceived, it bringeth forth sin: and sin, when it is finished, bringeth forth death.

James 1:14-15

Sin must be conceived, just a like a baby is conceived. A stork doesn't bring a baby, and you can't get pregnant by drinking "contaminated" water. Conception isn't something you catch from the germs of another person, like a cold. You have to plant that seed.

David began with a pure heart, a heart after God himself. Despite all of the hardships and challenging circumstances, David had remained faithful. While being pursued by his father-in-law, King Saul, he refused to be influenced by the ungodly counsel around him and stayed sensitive to the Lord. Throughout all of the battles and overwhelming circumstances, David kept his faith steadfastly in God. However, this episode with Bathsheba was an anomaly; it ran totally contrary to how his heart was most of his life.

David Lost His Vision

And it came to pass, after the year was expired, at the time when kings go forth to battle, that David sent Joab, and his servants with him, and all Israel; and they destroyed the

158

The Danger of Prosperity

children of Ammon, and besieged Rabbah. But David tarried still at Jerusalem.

2 Samuel 11:1

David was anointed by God to be king. Part of the king's job was to serve as commander-in-chief and supreme general over all the troops. As king, David should have gone out there with his armies and led in the battles. However he delegated this role to Joab, his highest-ranking general, and chose to stay home instead.

This is our first clue as to why David had this major moral failure. He wasn't doing what the Lord had called him to do. David had lost his vision. When you're under pressure, a hunger is stirred up on the inside of you to work harder to achieve your goals. When what you're pursuing seems almost out of reach, it keeps you intent and focused on the things of God. When you have a goal out in front of you, it keeps an energy and enthusiasm alive on the inside of you. But once you attain your goal, it is a dangerous time because you no longer have this purpose.

One of the things that made David such a great man was that he had a purpose that was bigger than himself. He served a higher purpose. He wasn't in it for himself. David's goal was to liberate God's people and bring the nation of Israel to the place of prominence and power that the Lord intended. He occupied himself with this as long as he saw himself as God's appointed minister and kept that goal out in front of him.

Lessons from David:

Bored

One of the best defenses against temptation is just being focused on what God has called you to do. Be occupied with your heavenly Father's business. It's very beneficial to have a purpose and a goal that consumes your time, energy, and attention. When you get bored, you open yourself up to many things from the devil.

As the popular saying goes, *Idleness is the devil's workshop.* Although this phrase is not in the Bible, I believe it's still a godly principle. You need to be doing something. You need to have a purpose, a goal and an aim for your life.

David had quit doing what God had called him to do. He had won many victories and the kingdom was now established. He had prospered and wanted to build God a temple, but the prophet had told him that one of his sons was going to do that. The Lord had given David tremendous prophecies concerning how his kingdom would endure, and that he would always have a son sitting on the throne. All of this brought David to an apex—he was at the top of his game. He had everything he wanted for the nation, for himself, and for his heirs. He had reached his goal and fulfilled what he set out to do.

He was so prosperous now that he could send his armies into battle without him at the helm. Besides, this was just a minor skirmish. It wasn't a major battle. There really wasn't any chance that Israel would lose this battle because they had superior power. Since victory was certain, David didn't have to go. He didn't have to do what God had told him to do.

160

Now that the pressure was off, David let up. He quit seeking the Lord with the same intensity he once had. Since he wasn't doing what God had told him to do, David basically became bored.

Hardship vs. Prosperity

And it came to pass in an eveningtide, that David arose from off his bed, and walked upon the roof of the king's house: and from the roof he saw a woman washing herself; and the woman was very beautiful to look upon.

2 Samuel 11:2

David was getting up out of bed when most people who have a job or a purpose are getting off work, going home, and going to bed! In other words, David wasn't doing anything. He wasn't overwhelmed with the affairs of the state. He was sleeping, napping during the day. David didn't have much to do because he had already reached his goal. That's a dangerous place to be!

Seasons of prosperity are more dangerous than seasons of pressure. When all of the pressure is removed and things are going well, you're most vulnerable to the devil. Conventional wisdom says that you will find out what's in someone when they're in difficult circumstances and under tremendous pressure. I disagree. Of course it takes faith and character to be able to persevere through hard times, but temptation is worse in times of prosperity.

In hardship, you know you need the Lord. When you're facing something overwhelming, it amplifies the reality of your need for God. You know you're incapable of dealing with the situation by yourself; it's bigger than you. Even someone with a low commitment to God will run to Him in hardship and ask Him for help. It's easy to seek the Lord and be God-dependent in a time of need.

Think about it. When do you pray the most? If you're like most people, you pray the most when you're under pressure. Trouble drives people to God! Anybody who knows He exists and that He wants to help them will turn to Him when the chips are down. But what happens when the pressure is removed?

What happened when everything was going so good that David could just send in his generals to fight the battle without him? He was so blessed and prosperous that he didn't have to strive anymore. David had the greatest mansion in all the land. He no longer had enemies breathing down his neck, trying to kill him every day. So David let up and began to coast. He stopped seeking God with the same intensity.

That's what caused David to commit this major moral failure. This wasn't just a mistake—an accidental, unintentional minor failure. This was a major departure from God, and it came as a result of choices. This sin was conceived over a period of time.

You Cannot Coast

This sin didn't really begin on the night David committed adultery with Bathsheba. It began months—possibly even years - before when David started being so blessed and prosperous that he wasn't driven to seek the Lord with the same intensity. He let his spiritual life slide. David probably became so occupied with the affairs of being king that before he knew it, a long time had passed since he had intimately related to God. That's really what caused this moral failure.

This is a warning to those of us who haven't done anything like this before. David was a man after God's own heart, yet look what he did! He committed adultery and even murdered Bathsheba's husband trying to cover up the affair. How far can you go? David loved God with all his heart, but here he was living in a way that even Saul never did. Many people whose stories we see in the Word of God who aren't considered as "great" examples, didn't live as bad a life as David did. How can someone do something like this? It just goes to show that the flesh is capable of doing anything, if you just let it go. You cannot coast!

When you're flying in an airplane, it seems so effortless. But if you turn off those motors, I can guarantee you that gravity is still pulling. You might think that because you've flown so long without any effort and everything has been working fine, that you can just do anything you want. However, I dare you to turn off those engines and see what happens. It's inevitable; you will come down!

It's the same way in the Christian life. You always have to keep the engines running seeking God and depending on Him. You can never get to a place where you don't want to have a better relationship with the Lord, wait on Him, and look to Him for everything. If you ever think you've arrived at such a place, you'll start to coast. If you ever become so prosperous and secure that you aren't seeking God and depending on Him, you're putting yourself in the most dangerous situation ever. Since your flesh is still capable of doing anything it ever could, it's just a matter of time before you fall. This ought to be a warning to you!

Instead of waiting until you have this great temptation or until some crisis hits, you need to learn to seek the Lord and keep your heart sensitive to Him right now. If you do that, you'll discover that you cannot wickedly depart from God unless you first of all depart from depending on Him. Even if you are prospering more than ever before, keep yourself aware of and acknowledging the truth that without God, you can do nothing. Your cry should be, "I need You every day of my life—not only when a crisis hits, but when everything is going good. Lord, I depend on You! I need You now just as much as ever before!" If you maintain this attitude, it will keep you from great transgressions.

Sins of Arrogance

David wrote:

Keep back thy servant also from presumptuous sins.

Psalm 19:13

The Hebrew word translated "presumptuous" literally speaks of sins of pride and arrogance. Pride is not just arrogance; it's self-sufficiency. When you are proud, you no longer humbly recognize your dependence on God. When everything is going good you think, *I've done all these things by my might and power.* You aren't recognizing your human frailty and need for God at all times. You need to say, "Keep us back from sins of arrogance. Keep us from operating independent of You, Lord!"

The Danger of Prosperity

Let them not have dominion over me: then shall I be upright,
and I shall be innocent from the great transgression.

Psalm 19:13

In this psalm, David said, "If You'll keep me from these sins of arrogance, from thinking I can make it on my own independent of You, that will keep me from a big fall. If you keep me in a situation where I recognize and acknowledge my dependence on You, that will keep me from the great transgression." You have to sin in the small areas of not seeking the Lord and being dependent on Him before you'll experience a big downfall. You have to sin by becoming arrogant, self-sufficient, and not being intimate with Him before you can enter into a great transgression.

These sins of adultery and murder didn't just jump on David. They had been coming on for months—perhaps even years—as he began to be so prosperous that he didn't have to depend on the Lord. He believed he didn't have to seek God the way he once did. That's where his sin was conceived. The adultery with Bathsheba and the murder of Uriah just happened to be the way his sin manifested itself.

Looking for Trouble

My teaching entitled, *How to Prepare Your Heart,* deals with this very thing. It explains why people do evil things and that these things don't just happen. In this teaching, I also share how you can keep yourself from entering this process simply by keeping yourself dependent on God. Humble dependence on the Lord makes all the difference!

165

Lessons from David:

David was so blessed and prosperous that he didn't feel compelled to do what the Lord told him to do. He wasn't obeying God. He was at home sleeping during the day, goofing off, aimless and purposeless. If you sleep all day and carouse at night, you're going to run into trouble. David was looking for trouble, and he found it!

Chapter 17

"You Are the Man!"

D avid saw Bathsheba, a beautiful woman, washing herself so he…

Sent and inquired after the woman. And one said, Is not this Bathsheba, the daughter of Eliam, the wife of Uriah the Hittite? And David sent messengers, and took her; and she came in unto him, and he lay with her; for she was purified from her uncleanness: and she returned unto her house. And the woman conceived, and sent and told David, and said, I am with child.

2 Samuel 11:3-5

When David found out Bathsheba was pregnant, he knew it was going to look really bad for him. His sin would be found out. But rather than humbling himself and dealing with his sin, he tried to cover it up. This reveals how hard David's heart had become toward God.

Lessons from David:

Sleeping on the Steps

David didn't miss a beat. He called for Bathsheba's husband, Uriah, to come back home. He was one of David's soldiers out fighting in the battles that David himself should have been fighting. David acted interested in the battle and what was going on with the troops out in the field. After Uriah gave him a report, David released him, expecting him to go home and have sexual relations with his wife. David even sent some food with him to bless him.

But it turned out that Uriah didn't go home. Instead, he stayed on the steps of the king's house. The next morning, David's men told him what Uriah had done, so David called Uriah in and asked, "Why didn't you go home last night?"

Uriah answered, "What am I going to do—go home and have relations with my wife while my comrades are out there sleeping on the ground and putting their lives on the line in battle? I will not do it!"

David saw that his plan didn't work so he had Uriah stay over some more. He had a feast and called Uriah to join him. David made Uriah drunk, thinking that surely his resolve would crack when he's drunk and he would then sleep with his wife. However once the feast was over, Uriah decided to stay there again at the steps of David's palace. Even though he was drunk, he refused to go home.

"You Are the Man"

Sin Always Affects Others

David finally realized that he wasn't going to be able to get Uriah and Bathsheba together, so he wrote a letter commanding his top general, Joab, to put Uriah in a place where he knew it was dangerous and then withdraw from him so that he would be killed. David even had Uriah deliver this letter to Joab himself! I'm sure the letter had some kind of seal on it for protection, but the king had seen that Uriah was a man of high standards and integrity. David probably had no doubt that the letter would be safely delivered. He sent Uriah's death sentence by his own hand. The irony, hypocrisy, and evil of David's plan is just amazing!

It's incredible to think that David could stoop so low. But David didn't do all this by himself. He had servants go out and bring Bathsheba to him. He had Joab, his general, comply with this plan. David involved other people in his sin. Many people say, "I'm not hurting anybody but myself by the things I do!" That's just never true. Somebody else is always hurt by our sin.

Once Joab executed David's order, he sent word back to the king. When David heard that Uriah was dead, he sent for Bathsheba and made her his wife.

> And when the mourning was past, David sent and fetched her to his house, and she became his wife, and bare him a son. But the thing that David had done displeased the LORD.
>
> *2 Samuel 11:27*

What an understatement! So Nathan—David's longtime friend,

Lessons from David:

advisor, and prophet—came to the king and told him a parable.

The Parable

And the LORD *sent Nathan unto David. And he came unto him, and said unto him, There were two men in one city; the one rich, and the other poor. The rich man had exceeding many flocks and herds: but the poor man had nothing, save one little ewe lamb, which he had bought and nourished up: and it grew up together with him, and with his children; it did eat of his own meat, and drank of his own cup, and lay in his bosom, and was unto him as a daughter.*

And there came a traveller unto the rich man, and he spared to take of his own flock and of his own herd, to dress for the wayfaring man that was come unto him; but took the poor man's lamb, and dressed it for the man that was come to him. And David's anger was greatly kindled against the man; and he said to Nathan, As the LORD *liveth, the man that hath done this thing shall surely die: and he shall restore the lamb fourfold, because he did this thing, and because he had no pity.*

2 Samuel 12:1-6

Of course, this was only a parable. It didn't really happen. It was symbolic of what David had done. David was like the rich man. God had blessed him and given him everything. Yet when he had a need, he didn't go to the Lord or draw from what He had already provided to meet that need. David had multiple wives. Second Samuel 3:2-5 lists six of them. In addition to these six and Michal

(2 Samuel 3:14), he also apparently had some concubines (2 Samuel 16:21-22). Therefore, David had at least seven wives that he could have gone to to satisfy his sexual desires. But instead of choosing one of these who were all legally his by law and given to him by God, David took another man's wife while that man was away serving the king and fighting his battle. Then David had that man killed in an effort to cover up his sin. That's what this parable was all about.

Mercy or Judgment?

David became furious and declared, "The man who has done this thing shall die! And he must also make four-fold restitution—give the poor man four lambs—for the one he took!"

In light of David's reaction, let's consider this scripture:

So speak ye, and so do, as they that shall be judged by the law of liberty. For he shall have judgment without mercy, that hath shown no mercy; and mercy rejoiceth against judgment.

James 2:12-13

The Lord delights in showing mercy to people who have shown mercy. But to those who have shown no mercy, who have been critical and judgmental instead, they will reap what they sow. David understood this principle. Although it's listed later in the chronology of the Bible, the words of the psalm contained in 2 Samuel 22 were spoken by David on the day the Lord delivered him from all his enemies, including Saul. David spoke these words before he became king and long before his sin with Bathsheba. Notice what he said:

Lessons from David:

With the merciful thou wilt show thyself merciful, and with the upright man thou wilt show thyself upright.

2 Samuel 22:26

In this passage, David basically said the same thing as what we find in James 2. He recognized that the Lord shows Himself merciful to those who have shown mercy, and with the upright, He shows Himself upright. At one time, David had had this principle revealed to him (see also vv. 27-28). He knew that if he wanted mercy, he had to show mercy. But if he didn't show mercy to other people, he in return would receive no mercy.

David Determined His Judgment

Yet David had quit seeking the Lord and had departed from Him. He had allowed himself to be drawn into adultery and, while trying to cover up that adultery, he committed murder. However, he was just going on as if nothing had happened.

David's heart had become so hardened that he had quit being responsive to the things God had shown him before. So when he heard this parable, he responded in judgment to a much lesser transgression than he himself had just committed. Taking another man's lamb and feeding it to a guest is nowhere near as great a transgression as taking another man's wife and murdering him to cover it up. David was the one in the greater transgression.

David basically determined his own judgment. The Lord gave him this parable through Nathan the prophet. David could have said, "This man did wrong, but I'm going to show him mercy.

Instead of giving him the punishment that he deserves, I'm just going to have him make restitution. Maybe his heart was right somehow." However, without asking for any further information or finding out any additional details, David jumped right into judgment declaring, "This man shall die! He's going to suffer four times the punishment for the suffering he caused." Mercy rejoices against judgment, but if you don't show mercy, you won't reap mercy!

God gave this parable to David to see how he would respond. Would he be merciful? If he had shown mercy, I believe the Lord would have been merciful toward him in the way He dealt with his transgression. But when David showed no mercy, he didn't reap any either. God responded to David the way he was responding to other people. David determined the harshness of his own judgment.

If we are merciful to others, we will receive mercy ourselves. I've done some stupid things, but since I've been merciful to others, I've been able to reap mercy. God has been gracious to me when I've said and done things that hurt other people's feelings, because I've been merciful to those who have hurt mine.

Are You Perfect?

I remember a certain media minister who was vicious and condemning toward anyone and everyone. When he fell, he received four-fold the judgment that he had put on other people. People were merciless with him and it destroyed his ministry. If he had shown more compassion toward others, he would have reaped more compassion in his time of need.

Lessons from David:

We all need to learn this lesson. If you want God to be merciful to you, you need to be merciful to others. If you rail on people when they make a mistake, you can expect to be railed on when you make a mistake. Is that really what you want?

We've all seen someone who thought they were Mr. or Ms. Perfect. They tried to make everyone else "perfect" like them, but if they weren't, they judged and criticized them. When this "perfect" person made a mistake and stumbled, you could see the vultures circling as if to say, "It's payback time. They've condemned me and everyone else. Now it's time they tasted some of what they've been dishing out!" You just love to see people like that receive what they deserve. But when someone has been merciful, you want to extend them mercy. That's just how things work!

David brought this judgment upon himself by being so strict in his criticism of the man in the parable.

And Nathan said to David, Thou art the man.

2 Samuel 12:7

This parable wasn't really about a rich man taking his poor neighbor's lamb. It was about David, Bathsheba, and Uriah. So Nathan declared to David, "You are the man!"

God Is Your Source

Thus saith the LORD God of Israel, I anointed thee king over Israel, and I delivered thee out of the hand of Saul; and I gave thee thy master's house, and thy master's wives into thy bosom, and gave thee the house of Israel and of Judah; and if that had been too little, I would moreover have given unto thee such and such things.

2 Samuel 12:7-8

The Lord was saying, "David, look what you've done! I've blessed you, prospered you, and done all these things for you. And if that wasn't enough, I would have given you more!" God was telling David that if he wasn't satisfied, He wasn't against him having more—more wives, more money, more fame, anything. The real sin wasn't adultery or murder; it was the fact that David quit trusting in the Lord. He stopped looking to God as his source.

At one time, David couldn't do anything. He was a poor and despised nobody, so he had to be dependent on God. However, once he became king, he was powerful. He was the head of one of the most powerful nations on the face of the earth at that moment. David could do anything he wanted, so he quit trusting in God as his supply. He started doing things just because he wanted to and could as king.

This is a real danger for us too. When we prosper to such a degree that we no longer have to pray and trust God to provide things for us because we can just go out and get anything we need or want on our own, beware! The danger is that we will quit depending on God as our source. That's really the transgression that the Lord was bringing out here. He was saying, "David, I would have given you more if you had asked Me!"

Lessons from David:

"You Despised Me"

Then Nathan continued:

Wherefore hast thou despised the commandment of the LORD, to do evil in his sight? thou hast killed Uriah the Hittite with the sword, and hast taken his wife to be thy wife, and hast slain him with the sword of the children of Ammon. Now therefore the sword shall never depart from thine house; because thou hast despised me, and hast taken the wife of Uriah the Hittite to be thy wife.

2 Samuel 12:9-10

Notice how the Lord reproved David. He didn't say, "David, look what you've done to Bathsheba—how you've defiled her. Look what you've done to Uriah—how you murdered him. Look at all of the people you've offended." No, that's not what the Lord said. The Lord was saying, "David, look what I've done for you. If you had trusted Me, I would have given you even more. But all of these things are going to happen now because you have despised Me." God said, "You despised Me!" This was all about David's personal relationship with God.

The Heart of Sin

Most people think of sin in terms of the damage done to others. Most people believe stealing is wrong because it violates and hurts the person they have stolen from. Since they look at it only in external terms, many folks justify certain types of theft.

Take for instance theft from an employer. Many people—even Christians—take pens and other small things from work. They'll steal a little bit of time, thinking *My employer has this big business, he can afford it!* So they doctor their time sheets and allow for a little bit of extra time. They don't feel bad about it because they're not thinking of what they've done as a sin such as stealing because of the relatively small amount of damage it is doing.

Some big corporations allow for a certain amount of thievery. They have insurance to cover fraud and other things like that. Some just write it off. So there's a bunch of people involved in what's called "white collar crime." They think, *I'm not doing anybody any damage. This corporation won't even miss $100,000. They have insurance to cover it.*

Even though the employees think about it in those terms, the issue isn't whether the company will miss it, has insurance to cover it, has made allowances for a certain amount of shoplifting, or whether they can get by with it. The issue is, the person committing these acts is sinning against God. They are despising the Lord! Instead of trusting God and letting Him supply them with things in an honest way, a way of integrity, they are going against Him and doing it their own way. Unbelief, not trusting God, is the heart of sin.

My teaching entitled, *The Positive Ministry of the Holy Spirit,* is taken from John 16:8-11. In verse 8, Jesus said that the Holy Spirit would reprove us of sin, righteousness, and judgment. Most people interpret this as saying that the Spirit reproves us of sins like adultery, lying, stealing, dope addiction, and other such things and then He tells us we're unrighteous because of what we did and if we don't repent, we're going to be judged. That's not at all what Jesus was saying. As a matter of fact, the Lord knew this verse would be misinterpreted, so He explained Himself in verses 9-11. The sin the Holy Spirit reproves us of is not believing on Jesus (unbelief, v. 9). The Holy Spirit doesn't convict us of "unrighteousness," but rather that we are righteous in Christ (v. 10). Verse 11 doesn't say that the Holy Spirit convicts us so we will be judged, but rather that He talks to us about the judgment of the devil. Religion has really twisted this up. Therefore, I strongly recommend this teaching. You'll be blessed!

Chapter 18

The Root of All Sin

The root of all sin is the fact that we aren't trusting God. That's really what's wrong with stealing. When someone steals, they aren't trusting God. It doesn't matter if a person or a corporation ever misses what was taken or not, God misses them depending on Him. They are going about obtaining their needs in an ungodly manner, contrary to His instruction. That's the transgression against God.

That's what's really wrong with sexual immorality and adultery. Even the church has fallen to the place where they reason against sin based on the physical consequences. They say, "If you sin sexually, you're exposing yourself to sexually transmitted diseases. And with today's AIDS epidemic and the prevalence of other sexually transmitted diseases, you're just playing Russian roulette!" They try to argue for sexual purity on the basis of just the possible physical consequences that could result from sexual promiscuity. Those things do exist and if that were all the reasoning you had, it would be good enough to remain sexually pure. It's just stupid to go out and do things like that. But at its core, this is really the wrong reasoning.

Lessons from David:

What would happen if medicine somehow came up with a cure for all sexually transmitted diseases? What if AIDS was obliterated? Would that all of a sudden make sexual promiscuity okay? Of course not! But if you use this kind of logic to convince someone that they shouldn't live in sexual immorality, they will be able to excuse it by saying, "I'm using protection. I'm having protected sex." They will just explain it away. However, the real root of sin is that they aren't trusting God.

Marriage Is Honorable

If you're married, the Lord gave you your mate.

Let thy fountain be blessed: and rejoice with the wife of thy youth. Let her be as the loving hind and pleasant roe; let her breasts satisfy thee at all times; and be thou ravished always with her love.

Proverbs 5:18–19

Marriage is honourable in all, and the bed undefiled.

Hebrews 13:4

In other words, God has purposed for you to satisfy your sexual desires with the marriage partner He gave you. Even from the very beginning, the Lord ordained that there should be one woman for one man. This was God's original plan. His plan for marriage is revealed in the fact that He made Adam and Eve—not Adam and Steve or Sue and Peggy. God didn't give Adam multiple wives. It was one woman for one man.

That's what's wrong with homosexuality. People argue against homosexuality saying you can get all of these diseases and the suicide rate among homosexuals is the highest of any segment of society. The real problem of homosexuality is that it rejects God's design. Homosexuals say, "I don't care what God did. I don't care what He says or what His will is. This is just the way I am!" No, it's not! They are rejecting and rebelling against God.

What would happen if a man's wife went out and committed adultery? What's really wrong with that? Well, you could talk about sexually transmitted diseases and ask, "What if she gets pregnant? What would happen to the child?" You could reason from all of these things, which are legitimate problems. But what if she did this and there was no sexually transmitted disease and no pregnancy that came of it. Just because there was an absence of physical consequences, would the husband say, "It's okay honey. You didn't pick up a sexually transmitted disease or become pregnant, so don't worry about it." Of course not! The real issue is that she broke her covenant with her husband. He would be grieved and have to deal with it.

It's the same way with God. Whether you get caught or experience any consequences in the natural isn't the issue. God knows that you aren't trusting in Him and looking to Him to meet your needs.

Lessons from David:

Broken Trust

That's what the Lord was telling David. He didn't say, "Look what you did to Bathsheba! Look what you did to Uriah! Look what it's going to cost you and the nation!" Instead He asked, "How could you have despised Me?"

When I first let my boys start taking the car to go on a date or some other outing, I'd tell them, "Be in by eleven o'clock." If they arrived home at 11:10, 11:15, or later, I'd ask them, "Why are you late?"

They would answer, "It's only ten or fifteen minutes. It's not a big deal."

Like most parents, I didn't always communicate things right. I remember saying, "It's late at night. What would have happened if you had a flat? Run out of gas? Gotten stuck or something? Nighttime is when all the weirdoes are out and about. It's dangerous. You could have been hurt. Something could have happened!"

This doesn't make much of an impact on kids. They don't believe they're going to run out of gas, have a flat, or whatever. But even if they believed that they might, they look at these consequences and wonder what the big difference is between 11 o'clock and 11:15. They just don't understand!

I might not have made this clear to my own children—it took me awhile to figure it out myself—but the real issue wasn't the possible consequences; it was a violation of my trust. It's not that in those fifteen minutes the whole world could turn bad and the car convert back into a pumpkin. The issue was that I didn't owe them anything. It was not a God-given right that they be allowed to drive the family car and stay out as late as they want. It was a privilege. I had extended grace to them and trusted them, but they didn't honor me. They offended me because they didn't honor my trust. If I said eleven o'clock, and they pushed it to 11:15, the real issue was that they'd broken my trust—not these other things.

The big deal is that they were trusted. By not honoring that trust, they show that they can't be trusted. They have proven that they don't really respect their parents and they're going to do whatever they want. And if their parents say eleven, they will push it fifteen minutes or so. That's the way it is with God. That is what's really wrong with sin.

It's Personal

You could argue that substance abuse is wrong because of its consequences. "Drugs and alcohol will damage your brain and your body. They will cost you money, and maybe even your job. You'll get into shame and be rejected." In reality, you're miserable and looking for an escape, willing to waste money and put your health on the line. You're saying that you are so miserable that you're willing to run all of these risks just for a few moments of being high, numb, and euphoric so you don't feel your problems. You're turning to a pill, a needle, or a bottle to alleviate your problems instead of turning to God. You're using this substance as a substitute for the Lord. That's what is offensive to Him. It's not just the health risk or the fact that you could have a car accident and kill someone.

Lessons from David:

These things are factors, but the root issue is that you aren't letting God meet your needs. You're trying to get them met some other way, and that's what grieves Him!

When you start looking at sin this way, it totally changes your perspective. The consequences no longer matter to you. Whether you can get by with something or not doesn't matter. It doesn't matter if anyone else is around or not. You have a personal standard on the inside of you that will hold you up in any circumstance because it's a personal deal between you and God.

That's how it was with Joseph. He was sold into slavery, bought by Potiphar in Egypt, and worked as a slave in his house. But because he was faithful to the Lord, God gave him favor. Joseph was promoted, but he caught the attention of his master's wife. She came and repeatedly tried to entice Joseph into committing adultery with her. Even though she pressed him, he wouldn't give in. Finally, one day Joseph declared:

How then can I do this great wickedness, and sin against God?

Genesis 39:9

If Joseph had been looking at his situation through eyes of moral relativity, applying "situational ethics," he could have reasoned, "I'm a slave. I was forsaken and sold into slavery. God hasn't done me any good!" In bitterness, he could have decided, "I'll just indulge myself. How could I ever get caught? Mrs. Potiphar certainly isn't going to tell her husband. That would put her own head on the line." If Joseph had only been looking at whether he could get by with this, he probably would have indulged himself.

184

The Root of All Sin

Stand Up or Stand Down?

But Joseph knew that though indulging himself with Potiphar's wife would have been a sin against Potiphar, the real issue was that it was a sin against God. This same logic kept me pure as a young American soldier in Vietnam while most of the other people I knew just lived like animals. I was in a company of two hundred guys and about once every six weeks, we had what was called "stand down." All of the frontline troops were brought to the rear for all of the booze and sex they wanted. They brought in Asian showgirls who were nothing but glorified prostitutes. After the "show," they would give them several bunkers so the men could have all the sex they wanted. Out of the two hundred guys in my company, I'm the only one I'm aware of who didn't participate!

One of the guys in our company was a fellow I had grown up with back home. We had even gone to the same church together. He wasn't a bad kid or anything like that, but when I talked to him about this activity, he just gave me the same logic that most guys used. He said, "I'm probably going to get killed next week anyway. What does it matter? I'm on the other side of the world and these are prostitutes. Nobody will ever know what I've done. Besides, everybody else is doing it!" Due to this reasoning, the vast majority of my fellow soldiers did things they wouldn't have normally done if they had been back home in the United States.

It didn't matter to me whether anybody else ever knew what I did or not, because God was there. I had a personal relationship with the Lord and I couldn't just sin against Him that way. That's what kept me from giving in.

Lessons from David:

God reproved David by saying, "David, how could you have done these things and despised Me?" That's what brought David back. The Lord didn't rebuke him based on consequences alone. God was saying, "David, at one time you loved Me!" The New Testament terminology for this is leaving your first love (Revelation 2:4). God was saying to David, "At one time, you used to adore Me. I satisfied you and gave you all these things. But now you've moved away from Me and you're satisfying your desires through lust, instead of love." That's the reasoning God used, and David got the message.

The Heart of the Matter

David repented of his sin with Bathsheba, as recorded in Psalm 51.

Have mercy upon me, O God, according to thy lovingkindness: according unto the multitude of thy tender mercies blot out my transgressions. Wash me thoroughly from mine iniquity, and cleanse me from my sin. For I acknowledge my transgressions: and my sin is ever before me. Against thee, thee only, have I sinned, and done this evil in thy sight: that thou mightest be justified when thou speakest, and be clear when thou judgest.

Psalm 51:1-4

Notice how David said, "Against You, and You only have I sinned." In one sense, that's not right. He sinned against Bathsheba and Uriah. He opened up a door for sexual sin and murder to work in his family. David caused a lot of trouble for many people. But these consequences were really only side issues. The heart of the matter was that David needed to repent and come back into proper relationship with God.

Lessons from David:

Chapter 19

Consequences

Although consequences aren't the main issue, they do exist. David's sin unleashed a barrage of negative consequences, and we would do well to learn from them.

Since David let this sexual immorality into his life, I believe it had access into his entire family. His firstborn son, Amnon, lusted after and raped his half-sister, Tamar (2 Samuel 13:1-20). Due to this Absalom, David's third oldest son and Tamar's full brother, became incensed at Amnon. It took him four years, but eventually Absalom brought vengeance upon Amnon and killed him (2 Samuel 13:28-29). So David opened up a door that allowed sexual sin and murder to influence his own children.

Absalom fled Jerusalem and lived in self-imposed exile for three years due to fear of what his father David might do (2 Samuel 13:38). When he finally came back, David still wouldn't talk to him for another two years (2 Samuel 14:21-24, 28). Absalom became upset and finally got an audience with his father, the king. David kissed him and hugged him, but apparently there wasn't total reconciliation (2 Samuel 14:33).

When his father didn't respond to him the way he wanted,

Absalom began a process of stealing the people's hearts away from the king and to himself (2 Samuel 15:6). David allowed this treason to go on unchallenged. Finally, Absalom tried to kill David and take over the kingdom. In the ensuing civil war, thousands and thousands of people died (2 Samuel 15-17).

When David fled Jerusalem as Absalom and his forces approached, he left some of his concubines behind to guard his house. Absalom set up a tent on the roof of the house, went in, and had sexual relations with his father's concubines in the sight of all the people (2 Samuel 16:22).

Although the main issue was David's relationship with God, his sin caused some major consequences for many people! It opened up his son to lust and, therefore, one of his daughters to rape. It opened up another son to murder. It caused a civil war. It also resulted in his own concubines being defiled in the sight of all the people. On and on the list could go!

Defiled and Destroyed

Ahithophel was the one who counseled Absalom to have sexual relations with his father's concubines (2 Samuel 16:20-21). Back then, when a new king took over a kingdom from another, it was customary for him to take the wives and/or concubines of the previous king and have sexual relations with them. The logic behind it was that if the previous king could have done anything about it, he would have. This signaled the fact that the previous king was out and the new king was in. It was a symbolic gesture demonstrating the total impotence of the previous king. It proved that the new king was now fully in power.

Although this was often customary, perhaps Absalom could have done something else to solidify the support of the people. Surely there was something else he could have done to communicate that this was a fight to the death with no chance of reconciliation. Why would Ahithophel—who was reputedly always right and never missed it—counsel Absalom to publicly defile David's concubines?

In 2 Samuel 23:34, the Bible reveals that Eliam was the son of Ahithophel. Over in 2 Samuel 11:3 (the passage where David's adultery is chronicled), Bathsheba is listed as "the daughter of Eliam." This would make Ahithophel Bathsheba's grandfather! From the very day when Ahithophel first saw David defile his granddaughter and kill Uriah, he nurtured bitterness and unforgiveness in his heart toward the king. While brooding over this for years and years, Ahithophel had been waiting for an opportunity to get even with David. I'm sure this contributed to his motivation to counsel Absalom in this way.

David's sin was costly! It let lust into Amnon and cost him his life. It cost Tamar her virginity. Absalom became bitter and caused a civil war. Ahithophel was polluted with unforgiveness. These concubines were defiled and their lives destroyed. All of these things were consequences of David's sin.

Lessons from David:

Man Conscious

Just because I'm emphasizing that the root of David's sin was his personal rebellion toward and lack of dependence upon God, doesn't mean that sin doesn't have consequences. Sin will take you further than you want to go, keep you longer than you want to stay, and cost you more than you want to pay. In light of the consequences alone, you don't want to sin. But you need to recognize and understand that sin is a transgression against the Lord. When you sin, you aren't trusting and believing God.

It doesn't matter if the people you steal from can afford it, are rich, and have insurance. The issue is that you aren't trusting God as your Source. You're doing it your way instead. You're imposing your wisdom above God's wisdom. It doesn't matter if you can commit sexual immorality without contracting a sexually transmitted disease, becoming pregnant, or getting caught. The issue is that you would be sinning against God.

This understanding will make a huge difference in your level of integrity. You'll get to where you operate in integrity whether anyone is watching, checking, or holding you accountable or not. Sad to say, most people don't live this way.

I actually read an article about some guys who put some money in a wallet and laid it on the sidewalk. In the wallet was a name and address, all the information needed to return the wallet to its original owner. They laid it on the sidewalk and then watched to see what people would do. Only about forty percent of the people actually operated in integrity and turned the wallet in. All the others just took it. When they did, the guys stopped them and asked them why they didn't turn it in. Most people answered, "If I had known someone was watching, I would have turned it in." In other words, situational ethics came into play. They thought, *Am I going to get caught? Will there be any consequences?* It's not because they were God-conscious. It's because they were man-conscious.

Serve the Lord

A person who is only doing what's right because it's expected of them and they're being held accountable for it, doesn't have a heart after God. True morality and integrity operates whether people see it or not. God's Word says we are to serve...

> *In singleness of your heart, as unto Christ; not with eyeservice, as menpleasers; but as the servants of Christ, doing the will of God from the heart; with good will doing service, as to the Lord, and not to men.*
>
> *Ephesians 6:5-7*

> *And whatsoever ye do, do it heartily, as to the Lord, and not unto men; knowing that of the Lord ye shall receive the reward of the inheritance: for ye serve the Lord Christ.*
>
> *Colossians 3:23-24*

In other words, it doesn't matter whether your employer knows that you are cutting your break short and working an extra five minutes. It doesn't matter whether you ever get rewarded from people or not. You need to boil everything down to doing it as unto the Lord, and not unto people.

Lessons from David:

My personal relationship with God is what kept me pure as a young soldier in the midst of many temptations in Vietnam. It didn't matter to me if my family or anybody else I looked up to knew what I was doing or not—God knew! And my relationship with Him caused me to have a level of integrity that most of the people over there at that time didn't have. What a powerful truth!

A New Covenant

There were reasons why David sinned. He quit having intimacy with God. It stopped being a personal relationship. He became so prosperous that he didn't have to seek God the way he did before, so he turned off his engines and began to coast. Without realizing it, he started sinking at that very moment. It was just a matter of time before some form of sin manifested. He committed adultery and then murder in an effort to cover up his adultery. Then David displayed a harsh judgment and because of that, God gave him the same judgment that he meted out.

Praise God for the New Covenant! All the judgment we deserved for our sins was placed upon Jesus two thousand years ago at the cross of Calvary. Now we have a better covenant based on better promises that was ratified through the shed blood of our Lord. Looking forward to this new covenant, David himself exclaimed:

> *Blessed is the man unto whom the LORD imputeth not iniquity, and in whose spirit there is no guile.*
>
> *Psalm 32:2*

Consequences

Paul even quoted this passage in Romans 4:8.

Blessed is the man to whom the Lord will not impute sin.

Under the Old Covenant, David had his sin imputed unto him. But you and I live in a covenant today where our sin has been imputed to Jesus. We aren't going to suffer judgment from God, but there is still much we can learn from this. Even though Jesus has borne our punishment, we should still abhor sin and walk in integrity, knowing that it cost our beloved Savior His life. He suffered. Every time you commit a sin, Jesus suffered that sin. I don't want to add to what the Lord has already borne. I want to live a life that glorifies God.

God's Grace Is Evident

David suffered the consequences for his sin. God forgave him, but the child born to Bathsheba died (2 Samuel 12:18). David interceded, thinking that maybe God would have mercy. But since David had shown no mercy, he received no mercy. The child died.

But you can still see the forgiveness and grace of God in David's life. He had sexual relations with Bathsheba again, this time they were lawfully married. Even though their whole relationship had been conceived in lust and sin, now that was over and repented of. God blessed their union and Bathsheba conceived a second son who lived. David called him Solomon, but God sent Nathan the prophet to rename him Jedidiah, which means beloved of the LORD (2 Samuel 12:24-25). God put His stamp of approval upon that marriage.

Lessons from David:

Now that's a powerful lesson for us. I've met many people who were married completely out of the will of God. The initial situation was totally ungodly, yet they found themselves in that marriage. What should they do now that they have turned their life over to the Lord? Should they divorce, cause a break, go find someone else, and complicate this thing?

The relationship of David and Bathsheba serves as a scriptural precedent. If you become born again in a totally ungodly marriage relationship, you—through your repentance—become a brand-new person. God sanctifies you. Just like David and Bathsheba, the Lord can make that relationship that was conceived in sin, godly. In fact, Solomon was chosen to be the next king. God's grace is evident throughout the entire life of David.

I encourage you to learn these life lessons at David's expense rather than through your own hard knocks. May these truths take root in your life so that you too will walk like David—as a man after God's own heart!

Conclusion

Remember that all the things recorded in scripture about David were to serve as examples for us (1 Corinthians 10:6, 11). Here is a brief summary of some of the lessons I've shared in this book.

• David wasn't God's first choice, yet look how powerfully God used him. He is still inspiring us over 4,000 years later.

• David's own family didn't see his potential, but God did and exalted him over those who were older and stronger. God saw his heart.

• David didn't let the persecution of others get him off track and up into the grandstands arguing with the spectators.

• David based his ability to succeed on God's covenant, not himself.

• David had confidence to fight Goliath because he had been faithful in smaller things.

• David fought until his enemy was dead, not just down.

• David was humble and depended on God, instead of himself.

• David was able to encourage himself in the Lord.

• David's great failures were a result of his prosperity. Success is a greater temptation than hardship.

- David didn't receive mercy, because he showed no mercy.

- David truly humbled himself and repented of his sins and continued to be used of the Lord.

- Although God totally forgave David, there were consequences to his sins that cost him and his family dearly.

These lessons I've learned through the life of David encouraged me to continue on in hard times and have saved me much heartache. I'm better off because of what I've learned through the good and bad experiences of David. I'm so thankful to the Lord for recording all of these things for my instruction. And I pray that you too will benefit greatly from the truths revealed in this book.

We all learn through our mistakes. I certainly have. But I've discovered a better way—to learn through someone else's mistakes. I pray the Lord will use these truths to enrich your life and cause you to prosper in Him as never before.

Receive Jesus
as Your Savior

C hoosing to receive Jesus Christ as your Lord and Savior
is the most important decision you'll ever make!

God's Word promises, "That if thou shalt confess with thy mouth the Lord Jesus, and shalt believe in thine heart that God hath raised him from the dead, thou shalt be saved. For with the heart man believeth unto righteousness; and with the mouth confession is made unto salvation" (Romans 10:9,10). "For whosoever shall call upon the name of the Lord shall be saved" (Romans 10:13).

By His grace, God has already done everything to provide salvation. Your part is simply to believe and receive.

Pray out loud: *Jesus, I confess that You are my Lord and Savior. I believe in my heart that God raised You from the dead. By faith in Your Word, I receive salvation now. Thank You for saving me.*

The very moment you commit your life to Jesus Christ, the truth of His Word instantly comes to pass in your spirit. Now that you're born again, there's a brand-new you.

Receive the
Holy Spirit

As His child, your loving heavenly Father wants to give you the supernatural power you need to live a new life. *For every one that asketh receiveth; and he that seeketh findeth; and to him that knocketh it shall be opened...how much more shall your heavenly Father give the Holy Spirit to them that ask him?*

Luke 11:10-13

All you have to do is ask, believe, and receive!

Pray: Father, I recognize my need for Your power to live a new life. Please fill me with Your Holy Spirit. By faith, I receive it right now. Thank You for baptizing me. Holy Spirit, You are welcome in my life.

Congratulations—now you're filled with God's supernatural power.

Some syllables from a language you don't recognize will rise up from your heart to your mouth. (1 Corinthians 14:14.) As you speak them out loud by faith, you're releasing God's power from within and building yourself up in the spirit. (1 Corinthians 14:4.) You can do this whenever and wherever you like.

It doesn't really matter whether you felt anything or not when you prayed to receive the Lord and His Spirit. If you believed in your heart that you received, then God's Word promises you did. "Therefore I say unto you, What things soever ye desire, when ye pray, believe that ye receive them, and ye shall have them" (Mark 11:24). God always honors His Word—believe it!

Please contact me and let me know that you've prayed to receive Jesus as your Savior or to be filled with the Holy Spirit. I would like to rejoice with you and help you understand more fully what has taken place in your life. I'll send you a free gift that will help you understand and grow in your new relationship with the Lord. Welcome to your new life!

About the Author

For over four decades, Andrew Wommack has traveled America and the world teaching the truth of the Gospel. His profound revelation of the Word of God is taught with clarity and simplicity, emphasizing God's unconditional love and the balance between grace and faith. He reaches millions of people through the daily *Gospel Truth* radio and television programs, broadcast both domestically and internationally. He founded Charis Bible College in 1994 and has since established CBC extension schools in other major cities of America and around the world. Andrew has produced a library of teaching materials, available in print, audio, and visual formats. And, as it has been from the beginning, his ministry continues to distribute free audio materials to those who cannot afford them.

To contact Andrew Wommack please write, e-mail, or call:

Andrew Wommack Ministries, Inc.
P.O. Box 3333
Colorado Springs, CO 80934-3333
E-mail: awommack@aol.com
Helpline Phone (orders and prayer):
719-635-1111
Hours: 4:00 AM to 9:30 PM MST

Andrew Wommack Ministries of Europe
P.O. Box 4392
WS1 9AR Walsall
England
E-mail: enquiries@awme.net
U.K. Helpline Phone (orders and prayer):
011-44-192-247-3300
Hours: 5:30 AM to 4:00 PM GMT

Or visit him on the Web at: www.awmi.net

Other Teachings by Andrew Wommack

Spirit, Soul & Body

Understanding the relationship of your spirit, soul, and body is foundational to your Christian life. You will never truly know how much God loves you or believe what His Word says about you until you do. In this series, learn how they're related and how that knowledge will release the life of your spirit into your body and soul. It may even explain why many things are not working the way you had hoped.

Item Code: 318   Paperback
Item Code: 1027-C   4-CD album

The True Nature of God

Are you confused about the nature of God? Is He the God of judgment found in the Old Testament or the God of mercy and grace found in the New Testament? Andrew's revelation on this subject will set you free and give you a confidence in your relationship with God like never before. This is truly nearly-too-good-to-be-true news.

Item Code: 308   Paperback
Item Code: 1002-C   5-CD album

The Effects of Praise

Every Christian wants a stronger walk with the Lord. But how do you get there? Many don't know the true power of praise. It's essential. Listen as Andrew teaches biblical truths that will spark not only understanding but will help promote spiritual growth so you will experience victory.

Item Code: 309   Paperback
Item Code: 1004-C   3-CD album

God Wants You Well

Health is something everyone wants. Billions of dollars are spent each year trying to retain or restore health. So why does religion tell us that God uses sickness to teach us something? It even tries to make us believe that sickness is a blessing. That's just not true. God wants you well!

Item Code: 1036-C   4-CD album

CHARIS BIBLE COLLEGE
COLORADO SPRINGS CAMPUS

2 Timothy 2:2
And the things that thou hast heard of me among many witnesses, the same commit thou to faithful men, who shall be able to teach others also.

Combining the rich teaching of God's Word with a practical hands-on ministry experience.

Two-Year Curriculum with an optional Third-Year School of Ministry Intern Program.

Night Classes
Distance Learning
Online & Correspondence
Available

For more information, call
Charis Bible College:
719-635-6029,
or visit our website:
www.charisbiblecollege.org
Ask about Extension School locations